VOID
Library
Davidson Colle...

ETHICS, POLITICS AND EPISTEMOLOGY:
A Study in the Unity of Hume's Thought

Aryeh Botwinick

University Press of America

Copyright © 1980 by

Aryeh Botwinick
University Press of America, Inc.

4720 Boston Way, Lanham, MD 20801

All rights reserved
Printed in the United States of America
ISBN: 0-8191-1288-7 (Case)
0-8191-1289-5 (Perfect)

192
H92xbo

Library of Congress Catalog Card Number: 80-5809

81-6541

"The impetus of reflection is not spent until we have restored in detail the unity of which we had a prevision."

Michael Oakeshott

For Imma

Shetichya Ad Meah V'Esrim Shanah

And to the Memory of Abba Z"L

Yehi Zichro Boruch

ACKNOWLEDGEMENTS

An earlier version of this essay served as my doctoral dissertation in political philosophy at Princeton University. My two readers for the dissertation -- Professor Sheldon Wolin of the Politics Department and Professor Thomas Scanlon of the Philosophy Department -- made many helpful criticisms and suggestions that have contributed in important ways towards the final result. I have also profited from discussion on Hume with Professors Manfred Halpern, Stuart Hampshire, Bruce Jennings, Alasdair MacIntyre, H.K. Miller, Paul Sigmund, Dennis Thompson, Robert Tucker and Margaret Wilson. Needless to say, I am alone responsible for all errors and shortcomings that remain.

TABLE OF CONTENTS

PRELIMINARY REMARKS xi

Chapter
I. MORAL JUDGMENT 1

    1. Meta-Ethical Doctrine 1
    2. Hume's Theory of Moral Judgment
       and the Doctrine of Sympathy 27
    3. Hume and Twentieth Century
       Ethical Theories 45

II. CAUSAL JUDGMENT 77

    1. Noncognitivism in Causal Judgment . . 77
    2. The Primacy of the Causal
       Relation 86
    3. Hume's Two Definitions of Cause . . . 92
    4. The Role of General Rules in
       Causal Judgment 99

III. POLITICAL THEORY 119

    1. Theory of Justice: Hume's
       Non-Utilitarianism 119
    2. Theories of Revolution and
       Political Obligation 139

IV. THE UNITY OF HUME'S THOUGHT 161

PRELIMINARY REMARKS

The purpose of the following essay is to explore the unity of Hume's thought. By "unity" I intend something very specific -- the utmost degree of coherence to which a piece of discourse on related topics can attain. If, according to one of its traditional definitions, philosophy as a mode of reasoning refers to a ceaseless pursuit of interconnections -- a relentless "reading out" of the implications of an argument, and judging how these affect the structure and ramifications of other phases of one's argument -- then a search for unity on a writer's part is coextensive with the philosophic enterprise itself. The role of an interpreter concerned with the question of unity would merely be then to ascertain how true to its philosophic ambition a piece of writing is. For purposes of better appreciating writings on politics, the identification of the mode of discourse in which they are written is important, since it forces us to discard erroneous preconceptions. If an author's intentions are practical, as Locke's for example were in the Second Treatise, we learn not to attack him for failing to attain the systematic coherence of Hobbes in Leviathan. The style of a political discourse is relevant for an understanding of the nature of that discourse: We revise our expectations to accord with the intentions of an author.

Hume's contribution to political theory is ostensibly written in a philosophical mode. It forms part of a larger work whose primary aim is to elaborate a science of man which encompasses "logic, morals, criticism and politics."[1] In the essay that follows, I have not sought to impose any external standard of coherence on Hume, but from a reading of Hume's philosophical program as he presents it in the Treatise I have tried to gauge the extent to which his philosophical practice measures up to his philosophical theory.

How philosophical a work is the _Treatise_? This is the primary question to which I shall be addressing myself in the following pages -- examining in detail some of Hume's major arguments in ethics, politics and epistemology in order to determine whether they contribute to or subvert his philosophical quest.

CHAPTER I

MORAL JUDGMENT

1. Meta-Ethical Doctrine

In Hume's ethical theory, strands which the historian of philosophy has learned to recognize as separate and in tension with each other cohere together in ways which challenge Hume's ingenuity to the utmost. A number of modern interpreters of Hume have used the famous "is-ought" paragraph,[2] in which Hume ostensibly shows the impossibility of deriving an evaluative conclusion from purely factual premises, as a basis from which to elaborate their own theories concerning "the essential Hume." It has been widely held that here, if anywhere, lies the key to Hume, and if only the statement and implications of the paragraph were gotten right, most other major difficulties in Hume would fall into place. While I share this view, I do not think -- for reasons that will become apparent in the pages which follow -- that the major interpretations that have been offered in this paragraph are satisfactory. In my discussion of Hume's ethics, I shall first set out the tensions in Hume's ethical theory which in a sense reach the breaking point in the "is-ought" paragraph, and then try to show how Hume resolves those tensions in the elaboration of his own positive ethical doctrine.

Hume's main arguments in the opening sections of Book Three of the Treatise -- which is devoted to ethics -- are directed against the ethical rationalists, whose writings constituted a powerful school of thought in England in the Eighteenth Century. With the waning of the influence of religion -- and the diminishing credibility evoked by supernatural sanctions for morality -- intellectuals were faced with the problem of providing a more naturalistic underpinning for the restraints imposed by morality.[3] In the debate that this large issue generated, Hume launched a skeptical attack against those who took the obvious step of arguing that natural reason enjoined those prohibitions which had previously been supported by a religious world view. Hume advances one major argument against the rationalists -- which, however, has a number of subsidiary facets -- and for the rest contents himself with posing the challenge that the rationalists' accounts of ethical judgment offered by his contemporaries were not satisfactory.

At the outset of Book Three, Hume invokes rigid empiricist criteria of knowledge in order to determine the origin of the distinction between vice and virtue. According to empiricist epistemological principles, in order for reason to be able to delineate this distinction it must be shown to reside either in some relation between ideas, or to be inferrable from some objective state of affairs. The bulk of Section One is devoted to showing that the first possibility must be ruled out, with the final two paragraphs of the Section arguing against the second possibility. Section Two of Part One, entitled, "Moral Distinctions Derived from a Moral Sense," was apparently intended to suggest the nature of Hume's solution to the problem of the origin of our moral distinctions.

Hume relies upon and further buttresses his arguments in Book Two, Part Three, Section Three of the <u>Treatise</u> -- entitled "Of the Influencing Motives of the Will" -- in order to attack the position that moral distinctions betoken exclusively relations between ideas. In Book Two, Hume had delineated the respective provinces of reason and passion, or will. Starting again with the empiricist criteria of knowledge which he had elaborated and defended in Book One of the <u>Treatise</u>, criteria which state that reason can inform us only of two kinds of truth -- demonstrative or mathematical truth which consists solely in unfolding the relations between ideas, and probable truth which rests on causal inferences between matters of fact -- Hume argues that neither of these sources of knowledge can actuate the will. Demonstrative reasoning is restricted in scope to mathematics and therefore cannot influence practical affairs. Even where mathematics is applied in daily life, such as a merchant adding up the amount of money due his creditors, mathematics only helps one to implement the means towards an end that was chosen on other than mathematical grounds.

Concerning reason's role in helping us to elaborate causal inferences with regard to matters of fact, it is obvious, Hume claims, that this role would never come into play if there were not some antecedent force propelling it into operation. The antecedent forces for Hume are pain and pleasure -- the prospect of pain impelling us to discover the means necessary to avoid it, and the possibility of pleasure luring us on to augment the means necessary to attain it. Reason's role in both cases is thus intermediary -- working to fashion means to ends that have been determined on other grounds.

According to the dualistic metaphysics shared by Hume and his contemporaries, a diminishing of the role played by reason meant an enhancement of the part contributed by passion. Passions, for Hume, are "original existences"[4] which arise spontaneously in man and affect his behavior. One can give the generic name of pleasure to all those impulses which draw man into their orbit, getting him to move towards or to achieve certain ends. Conversely, the generic name pain is given to those impulses which threaten man, and which he seeks to avoid. Since passions are "original existences" -- not owing their presence within the soul of man to any other source but themselves -- they cannot be opposed by reason but only by other passions. Reason's role in this scheme is entirely subservient -- it either helps define more clearly the object of one's attraction or repulsion, or determines the most effective means of achieving what one wants or avoiding what one seeks to avoid. Outside this instrumental sphere, reason is impotent, being outflanked by "original existences" whose role within the human economy is to establish the ends of one's behavior.

Hume builds on his picture of the respective functions of reason and the passions when he comes to deal with the question of the foundations of moral judgment. Since only passions excite us to action, moral judgments whose ostensible subjects are actions cannot be based on reason. Should one grant Hume's premises about the division of labor between reason and the passions and nevertheless claim that immorality consists in the factual errors that one makes concerning the desirability of certain ends and of the proper means to achieve them, Hume would respond by pointing out the absurdity of the position that one is left to defend. With virtue consisting in conformity to reason in the sense thus narrowly defined, all the factors which the common sense of humanity regards as crucial to the framing of moral judgments -- such as whether the object of the judgment be animate or inanimate; whether the error be avoidable or not; and the question of degrees of blame to be apportioned -- would have to be excluded as falling outside the pale of moral judgment.

Hume's account of the relationship between reason and the passions has proven very persuasive with Twentieth Century ethical philosophers, mainly emotivists and prescriptivists. Following Amelie Rorty, we might designate this strand of Hume's ethical thought as "psychological noncognitivism."[5]

The term refers to the subservient role assigned to reason in Hume's schema of the relationship between reason and the passions, and also to reason's impotence in helping us determine outside a framework of ends previously ordained by our passions which course of action to pursue. Hume now proceeds in the remaining part of Section One to refute specific rationalist positions that were current in his day. These arguments for the most part are vitiated, so to speak, on a double level. The rationalist arguments themselves are in most cases quite feeble which detracts from the strength Hume's arguments might have, since they are mainly demolishing straw men. Secondly, Hume's counter-arguments considered in their own right are not very persuasive. Nevertheless, this portion of Section One is important for our purposes since it reveals further aspects of the constraints Hume sets on a positive theory of moral judgment.

In a famous footnote,[6] Hume considers the position of his contemporary Wollaston. Wollaston has argued that the root-source of immorality lies in the tendency of any action so designated to give rise to a falsehood in the eyes of a spectator. Thus, if I act ungenerously towards my benefactor, my action is immoral because it creates the impression among un-knowledgeable observers that this particular person is not my benefactor, which is a falsehood. Hume deploys several arguments against Wollaston: First, he argues, that if being the occasion of a false inference provides the root notion of immorality, then whenever our judgment is faulty, and we draw an erroneous inference concerning a matter of fact, whatever occasioned that false inference, even if it be an inanimate object, would be the valid subject of moral blame. Second, Hume points to other absurd conclusions to which a consistent follower of Wollaston's doctrine would be led. According to Wollaston's theory, if I had managed to conceal from public view my ingratitude to my benefactor, I would have been guilty of no immorality whatsoever. Third, Hume claims that Wollaston's argument is circular. A person who acts unkindly towards his benefactor in a manner affirms that this person is not his benefactor. But in what manner, Hume asks, does his behavior affirm this? Is it because of a duty of kindness towards one's benefactor? In that case, acting in violation of the antecedent duty constitutes the immorality, and Wollaston has not established that acting kindly towards one's benefactor is a duty. Fourth, extending the previous argument, Hume says that Wollaston's case falters because he fails to show that acting in such a manner as to spread falsehood is itself immoral: "I shall allow if you please that all immorality is derived from this supposed falsehood in action, provided you can give me any plausible reason why such a falsehood is immoral. If you consider rightly of the matter, you will find yourself in the same difficulty as at the beginning." Hume adds that "this last argument is very conclusive."

Continuing his arguments against those who would establish morality on a purely rational basis, Hume challenges his opponents to set forth those relations between ideas on which morality might be rested. Hume cites from his epistemology the four relations between ideas which yield certainty -- resemblance, contrariety, degrees in quality and proportions in quantity and number -- and indicates that since these relations hold indiscriminately between inanimate objects, actions, passions and volitions, they cannot serve as the basis of moral judgments which refer uniquely to the latter three.

Hume now considers the two conditions which rationalists would have to meet in order to establish a basis for morality, and which he claims it would be impossible for them to meet. First, they would have to discover a relation between ideas in addition to the four enumerated above which applied exclusively to ideas of the relationship between passions and volitions and action, and would not apply to the passions and volitions considered among themselves, or to actions considered among themselves. If the relation suggested encompassed the latter two categories, it would fall prey to the absurdity of rendering someone immoral simply for what transpired inside the confines of his own skin between certain thoughts and emotions, and of allowing relationships of morality and immorality to subsist between inanimate objects in nature.

The second condition that rationalists would have to meet would be to show that the relations between ideas which they discovered to be the foundation of morality bore an immutable relation to the will, providing some motivation on the part of all individuals to perform or refrain from performing the course of action enjoined or prohibited. Since according to Hume's analysis of causality even the relation between our desiring to lift our hand and lifting it is a contingent one, revealed to us only in the light of experience,[7] the rationalist hope of establishing the relationship between a particular course of action and the will on an a priori basis can be shown to be illusory from the start.

Amelie Rorty identifies a separate strand of semantic noncognitivism in Hume, which she bases upon the two examples which Hume invokes in illustrating his case against the rationalists.[8] If the evil of patricide, Hume suggests, resided solely in the relation subsisting between father and son which made commiting this crime particularly heinous, then a similar relation existing between an oak and an acorn should taint the "action" of the acorn in overtowering the oak with an equal degree of guilt. A rationalist could not distinguish between the two cases by saying that the presence of will in the former case, and its absence in the latter, constituted sufficient grounds for denominating the former action evil and withholding moral judgment from the latter. Since the evil inheres entirely in the relation, the presence of will in the case of a son murdering his father could only be the cause why a relation of moral evil arises between human beings, but could not increase or detract from the degree of guilt which the action itself occasions. Rorty interprets this passage as containing in embryonic form C. L. Stevenson's distinction between descriptive and emotive uses of language.[9] Hume's argument that there is no fixed connection between the words "good" and "evil" and particular courses of action can be read as a statement about language itself. There are no determinate descriptive meanings to the words "good" and "evil," only a floating content annexed by individual users of a language to suit their needs and purposes. Only the emotive meaning remains constant in the manifold contexts in which the terms "good" and "evil" are employed.

The second counter-example which Hume adduces against the rationalists is that of incest, which evokes moral guilt when practiced between human beings but not between animals. Again, an attempt to distinguish between the two cases -- by saying that human beings possess reason and can therefore be held morally culpable, whereas animals do not, rendering moral epithets wholly inappropriate when applied to them -- would have to fail. If moral judgments were pronounced solely on the basis of relations residing between things, this would mean that reason was only instrumental in discovering these relations, but not that it had created them. These relations would exist independently of reason, and would pervade the whole universe and not be restricted to man.

So far in this section Hume has been arguing against those who would base moral judgments on some exercise of demonstrative reason. In the penultimate paragraph of the section, Hume deals with those who would found moral judgment on an exercise of the practical reason which draws probable inferences concerning matters of fact. His argument against them is simple. He asks them to consider an act such as willful murder and to determine what sorts of probable inference one can draw from the act. The only inferences could be to such entities as passions, motives, volitions and thoughts. As long as one considers only the objective state of affairs -- a certain man lifted a revolver and shot another human being -- no inference to a moral judgment is possible.

In the final paragraph of Section One, of Part One, of Book Three Hume imposes an additional constraint on an adequate theory of moral judgment beyond those we have already considered. In the famous "is-ought paragraph," what one might delineate as a non-naturalistic strand[10] in Hume's thought emerges into clear focus.

> I cannot forbear adding to these reasonings an observation, which may perhaps be found of some importance. In every system of morality which I have hitherto met with I have always remarked that the author proceeds for some time in the ordinary way of reasoning, and established the being of a God, or makes observations concerning human affairs; when of a sudden I am surpriz'd to find that instead of the usual copulations of propositions is and is not I meet with no proposition that is not connected with an ought or ought not. This change is imperceptible; but is however of the last consequence. For as this ought or ought not expresses some new relation or affirmation, 'tis necessary that

it should be observed and explained; and at the same time that a reason should be given, for what seems altogether inconceivable, how this new relation can be a deduction from others, which are entirely different from it. But as authors do not commonly use this precaution, I shall presume to recommend it to the readers; and am persuaded that this small attention would subvert all vulgar systems of morality and let us see that the distinction of vice and virtue is not founded merely on the relations of objects nor is perceived by reason.[11]

The traditional interpretation of this paragraph[12] takes Hume as arguing for an unbridgeable logical gap between descriptive premises and an evaluative conclusion. It is not irrational for a disputant according to Hume to concede the factual premises of his opponent while denying the evaluative conclusion. In order for the descriptive premises to entail the conclusion, some intervening premise would be required, the nature of which Hume does not specify.

The difficulty with the received interpretation, however, is that Hume's own version of a valid moral argument -- even as he summarized it briefly in the paragraph preceding the "is-ought paragraph" -- seems to conflict with the logical canon enshrined by the classical reading of "is-ought." In the penultimate paragraph of Section One, Hume says that

The vice entirely escapes you as long as you consider the object. You never can find it, till you turn your reflexion into your own breast, and find a sentiment of disapprobation which arises in you towards this action. Here is a matter of fact; but 'tis the object of feeling, not of reason. It lies in yourself, not in the object. So that when you pronounce any action or character to be vicious, you mean nothing but that from the constitution of your nature you have a feeling or sentiment of blame from the contemplation of it. Vice and virtue therefore may be compared to sounds, colors, heat and cold which according to modern philosophy are not qualities in object, but perceptions in the mind: And this discovery in morals, like that other in physics, is to be regarded as a considerable advancement of the speculative sciences; tho' like that too it has little or no influence on practice. Nothing can be more real or concern us more than our own sentiments of pleasure and uneasiness; and if these be favorable to virtue, and unfavorable to vice, no more can be requisite to the regulation of our conduct and behavior.[13]

In apparent contradiction of the "is-ought" paragraph" which immediately follows, Hume in the above passage seems to derive moral judgments directly from a statement indicating the presence of certain feelings of pleasure or pain in man.[14] To make the "is-ought paragraph" accord with Hume's philosophical practice has therefore been the object of many of the modern re-interpretations of the paragraph. Alasdair MacIntyre in an article entitled "Hume on 'Is' and 'Ought'"[15] turns the received interpretation on its head, and reads Hume as saying that a deduction from factual premises to an evaluative conclusion is possible. The crucial words which he regards the traditional interpretation as misconstruing are: "for what seems altogether inconceivable, how this new relation can be a deduction from others." The first phrase was read ironically -- the word "seems" was not taken literally -- and the second phrase was read literally -- "deduction" was taken to mean strict entailment. MacIntyre argues that the reverse should be the case -- "seems" should be read literally, and "deduction" should be interpreted broadly to mean simply inference. Read in this way, Hume would be understood as saying that an inference from a factual premise to an evaluative conclusion can be drawn if one abandons the model of strict entailment. A nonevaluative middle premise that can support an evaluative conclusion according to MacIntyre's reading of Hume would be one that stated that a particular course of action represented what the common consensus regarded as furthering the public interest. MacIntyre says that the requirement of an additional evaluative premise to the effect that whatever is in everyone's long-term interest should be done would be redundant for Hume, because the notion of consensus of interest just forms an essential part of what the word "ought" means.

 A major flaw in MacIntyre's account consists, I think, in his ignoring the literal import of the "is-ought paragraph." Read literally, the paragraph states that one cannot move from a factual premise to an evaluative conclusion without introducing some intervening non-factual premise. That this is not an isolated belief on Hume's part but forms an integral part of his case against the rationalists is evidenced by his utilizing the argument against Wollaston in the famous footnote summarized earlier. There Hume pointed out that there was a circularity in Wollaston's account of morals, since in order to show that giving rise to a falsehood was at the root of all our designations of things as evil Wollaston would first have had to show that lying itself is evil. The proper form of moral argument that seems to emerge from Hume's critique of Wollaston is the following:

Falsehoods should not be perpetrated

This particular action gives rise to a falsehood

. . this particular action should not be done.

A second major re-interpretation of the "is-ought paragraph" has been given by Geoffrey Hunter, who follows the lead of Professor Gilbert Ryle.[16] Hunter allows the two phrases that MacIntyre re-interpreted to stand exactly as they were in the traditional view, while claiming that the context of Hume's moral philosophy makes clear his intention in the "is-ought paragraph." The logical gap between factual premises and evaluative conclusion that the received interpretation points to makes moral judgment impossible only if one believes that to utter a moral judgment is to make a non-factual statement. The whole point of Hume's moral philosophy, however, is to indicate the factual basis of moral judgments, that all they simply do is report a particular agent's feelings concerning certain objects or states of affairs. What the paragraph underscores is the logical problem that religious moralists, say, face when they regard moral judgments as something other than an agent's stating his feelings when confronted by a particular situation.

Hunter himself voices a most serious criticism against his analysis of Hume's theory of moral judgment when he says that according to his account Hume becomes incapable of explaining ethical disagreement.[17] If all one does in making a moral judgment is report on his emotional reaction to a contemplated course of action, say, then it is entirely possible for two disputants to admit to each other that their opponent's feelings move them in ways directly contrary to their own feelings, thus effectively preventing ethical disagreement from ever getting off the ground.

Also, Hunter, like MacIntyre, in ignoring the literal import of the paragraph, fails to do justice to a key element in Hume's argument against the rationalists.

In trying to determine to what extent the account of morals in the Enquiry Concerning the Principles of Morals diverges from or expands upon the argument found in the Treatise, we are afforded an insight, I believe, into how to construe the "is-ought paragraph" in a way that will both accommodate Hume's criticism of the rationalists as well as rendering intelligible his own theory of moral judgment. The Second Enquiry, as far as I can tell, refines the argument in the Treatise mainly in two ways. First, though Section Two of Part One of Book Three of the Treatise is entitled "Moral Distinctions Derived from a Moral Sense," the notion of a separate moral sense practically disappears from view once we get into the body of the argument. What Hume argues for in the Section itself is the equation of the feelings we experience in disinterestedly contemplating the harmful or beneficial results of certain tendencies of character or states of affairs with the moral distinction between good and evil. In Section One of the Second Enquiry, on the other hand, Hume is quite explicit about the independent status of the moral sense. He says that "this final sentence (of approbation or censure) depends on some internal sense or feeling, which nature has made universal in the whole species. For what else can have an influence of this nature?"[18] Apparently, in order to satisfy his readers -- and perhaps himself -- of the truly scientific, i.e. universal, character of his explanation of the foundation of moral judgment, Hume felt compelled in the Second Enquiry to regard the mechanism of approval and disapproval described earlier in the Treatise as the manifestation of a special moral sense implanted in the species by the Designer of Nature.

A second elaboration which emerges in the Second Enquiry occurs in Appendix I, and is contained in the following two paragraphs:

> It appears evident that the ultimate ends of human actions can never, in any case, be accounted for by reason, but recommend themselves entirely to the sentiments and affections of mankind without any dependence on the intellectual faculties. Ask a man why he uses exercise; he will answer because he desires to keep his health. If you then enquire why he desires health he will readily reply because sickness is painful. If you push your enquiries farther, and desire a reason why he hates pain, it is impossible he can ever give any. This is an ultimate end, and is never referred to any other object.
>
> Perhaps to your second question, why he desires health, he may also reply, that it is necessary for the exercise of his calling. If you ask why he is anxious on that head he will answer because he desires to get money. If you demand Why? It is the instrument of pleasure says he. And beyond this it is an absurdity to ask for a reason. It is impossible there can be a progress in infinity; and that one thing can always be a reason why another is desired. Something must be desirable on its own account, and because of its immediate accord or agreement with human sentiment and affection.[19]

Hume's argument here, I believe, is crucial to an understanding of his views on moral judgment, and indeed of the structure of argument in his philosophy as a whole. It is very easy to misinterpret Hume in this passage. One might think that he is making the rather innocuous-sounding logical point that in order to avoid an infinite regress an argument must stop somewhere, and he has found it most plausible to rest his argument in morals with a statement to the effect that a particular type of character or state of affairs is most conducive to pain or pleasure. Viewed in this light, the argument is singularly un-persuasive, because we are not told why we should stop at this particular resting-place. We have escaped an infinite regress only at the cost of an arbitrariness that may leave us equally dissatisfied.

I believe that if read correctly Hume in this passage does meet the charge of arbitrariness by moving the argument on to a different level. The crucial phrases in the passage in my view are "but recommend themselves entirely to the sentiments and affections of mankind, without any dependence on the intellectual faculties" -- in the first paragraph -- and "Something must be desirable on its own account, and because of its immediate accord or agreement with human sentiment and affection" -- in the second paragraph. These words should be construed entirely literally. The reason why a statement concerning an object's conduciveness towards pain or pleasure can serve as an ultimate statement in an argument is because when we speak the language of pain or pleasure we are no longer speaking the pure language of reasons, but have introduced the idiom of causes, i.e., the idiom of universal connection. We are so constituted that we want to avoid pain, and seek whatever affords us pleasure. The feelings of pleasure and pain that precede and accompany the utterance of a moral judgment conform to the general rules Hume lays down for identifying genuine causal relations from mere haphazard connections in nature.[20] The feelings of pleasure and pain are contiguous in time with the

judgment and are always experienced prior to it.
A constant union is evident between the cause
and the effect, and we can say with pragmatic
certainty that the same cause always produces
the same effect and the same effect never arises
but from the same cause. Thus without experiencing the conjunction on any particular occasion
we are licensed to predict according to Hume on
the basis of the evidence that we have that the
feeling will produce the judgment.

The object of Hume's criticism in the passages quoted above from the <u>Second Enquiry</u> is
any justificatory mode of argument which seeks
to base itself on the language of reasons. The
inevitability of an infinite regress does not
undermine any particular set of reasons, but the
very language of reasons itself. One cannot offer
a decisive argument in morals, or elsewhere,
simply by citing reasons for the choice one is
defending, because one's choice of reasons is
always open to the further question "Why?" which
can never logically be foreclosed. To avoid this
regress one must shift the level of argument to
a plane which precludes the intrusion of personal
judgment, desire or reasons. This is the plane
of scientifically ascertainable causes, which
exhibit a universal correlation between certain
sentiments in man and particular states of affairs.
This is a case of science forestalling the endless
disquisitions of reason, by pointing to what is
objectively verifiable and universally present.

My interpretation of Hume in these two crucial paragraphs in Appendix I to the <u>Enquiry</u> is
predicated upon the dual assumption that a purely
causal account of human actions is possible, and
that a general distinction between reasons and
causes as applied to human action can be drawn.
Since both issues have been the focus of much
discussion in recent philosophical literature,
I must at least show what arguments might be

adduced to render the making of these two assumptions plausible.

The notions that actions may be caused has a venerable pedigree in traditional philosophical literature.[21] The agency that causes the action is pictured as a mental act -- namely, willing. Hobbes, for example, in a famous definition, describes willing as follows: "In deliberation, the last Appetite, or Aversion, immediately adhering to the action, or the omission thereof, is what we call the Will; the Act (not the faculty) of Willing."[22] Hume's definition of the will echoes Hobbes: "I desire it may be observed, that by the will I mean nothing but the internal impression we feel, and are conscious of when we knowingly give rise to any new motion of our body or new perception of our mind."[23] Kant introduces the conceptual innovation that in order to qualify as an act of will the deliberation preceding action must be in accordance with universal principles: "Everything in nature works according to laws. Rational beings alone have the faculty of acting . . . according to principles, i.e., have a will."[24] It is important to note two aspects of the traditional doctrine of acts of will which have come in for attack by Twentieth Century analytic philosophers. First is the idea that in order for anything to qualify as an action it must be preceded by a separate mental act of deliberation and decision. Second, since deliberation and action are kept distinct, the relation between them is always contingent, and never necessary.

Gilbert Ryle, in The Concept of Mind,[25] has done more than any other contemporary philosopher to undermine the dualistic picture of mental life upon which the traditional doctrine of the will rested. Chief among his arguments which relate to the notion of the will are the following:

1. Ryle follows a criteriological principle which is also shared by Wittgenstein. Ryle believes that the meaning of a term is exhausted when the criteria for its application are indicated. Since in the case of so-called mental action verbs, such as willing or desiring, the criteria for their application all refer to success or failure in overt performance, it becomes sheerly redundant to postulate mental entities over and above the physical manifestations of these "mental acts."[26]

2. Specifically, Ryle argues that deliberation cannot be the mental event that the traditional doctrine focused upon as a sine qua non of action. Since we agree to call by the name of action even what takes place without prior resolution, the traditional doctrine's insistence that something cannot be classified as an action if it is not preceded by an "act of deliberation" can be empirically shown to be false.[27]

3. Ryle places great stress on the argument that such descriptions of actions with mental overtones as "voluntary," "responsible," "done on purpose," and "accidentally" are adjudged true or false merely by reference to overt behavior. We look to the actual performance in order to determine whether these adjectives apply or not, and do not seek to inspect the acts of will which according to the traditional doctrine sparked the performance.[28]

4. In ordinary discourse, no one ever talks about his acts of volition. Reference is made to such entities as actions, gestures, qualms and embarrassments -- whose criteria of application, moreover, are in each case overt -- which apparently suffice to do the job of work that traditional philosophers ascribed to volitions.[29] One implication that might be drawn from Ryle's dispositional analysis of mental action verbs is

19

that he makes them more easily manipulable objects
of a possible causal explanation -- since both
explanadum and explanans would refer to overt
manifestations of behavior -- than they would
be interpreted in the more literal language of
the traditional doctrine.

An additional argument which has been widely
regarded as effective in undermining the traditional role assigned to volitions has been presented by A.I. Melden in his book Free Action.[30]
Melden states that to argue as the traditional
theorists have done is to be involved in an infinite regress. If an act of will is itself an
action, then it requires a preceding act of will
in order to be performed -- which repeats itself
at each stage, and prevents the notion of an act
of will preceding action from ever getting off
the ground.

Ryle's arguments against postulating a separate category of volitions have helped provide
the keynote for the anti-behaviorist argument.[31]
Where Ryle has attacked volitions as mental causes,
the anti-behaviorists have extended his arguments
and turned them against him to launch an attack
on the whole notion of causality when applied
to human actions. They have sought to show that
in speaking of human actions we are introducing
a separate dimension of experience, where only
the language of reasons is appropriate.

Among the prominent arguments laying the
groundwork for the application of separate criteria of reasons to action have been the following:

1. The criteria for the application of terms
relating to bodily movements are not the same
as those for the performance of actions signified
by those bodily movements. Thus, for example,
the same bodily movement is involved in the three
different actions of signing a check, giving an

autograph and authorizing an agent to do something in one's behalf. Obviously, the criteria appropriate for determining whether certain bodily movements took place bear no resemblance to the criteria that would have to be invoked to determine whether any of the above mentioned actions took place.

2. The predicates appropriate to answering questions about human actions are of a different logical order from the predicates appropriate to answering questions about bodily movements. Thus, if someone were to ask me why my hand moved, the appropriate answer would include reference to conditioned reflexes, muscles and nerves. If someone were to ask me, however, why I moved my hand, an appropriate answer would include reference to my reasons, goals, intentions or purposes. Also, as a corollary to this, when the question is why I moved my arm, I possess a unique authority in answering which stems from my usually being in a better position to know than anybody else what reasons, purposes or goals motivated my behavior. When the question, however, is asked about why my arm moved I have no special authority in answering the question, and must defer to the expertise of the physiologist.

3. When I refer to an action that I did there is no room for the further question, how do you know? Raising such a question has point where the relevant criteria that are appealed to can be placed along a sliding scale indicating varying degrees of certainty. Thus, in raising the question whether it rained yesterday, answering in terms of memory, a weather report in today's paper or a letter from a friend might be shown to carry varying degrees of certainty. Where self-knowledge of my own present actions is at issue, my knowledge is not one of degree. Where bodily movements are concerned, however, since objective observations by myself or others

are always in place, so too are varying degrees of knowledge, and consequently the question, how do you know? retains its appropriateness.

4. Where I talk about a proposed action, using the future tense, the statement that I make is classifiable as an expression of intention and not as a prediction. Even where I use knowledge of my own intentions to make a prediction about my behavior, knowledge of my intentions forms the prior step which makes prediction possible. Where bodily movements are concerned, however, the notion of intention is completely out of place, and only the language of prediction is appropriate. One can make safe predictions about a person's bodily movements even without any knowledge of his intentions.

5. The point of the distinction between bodily movements and action comes out most clearly perhaps in those ambiguous situations in life where we are uncertain about how to classify what happened. We decide to act in a certain way before a particular situation arises, but then when we are confronted by the actual circumstances, we act contrary to our original intentions. In retrospect, we are unsure how to describe what happened. We say such things as "My lips seemed to move of their own accord. I was not aware . . . I was not responsible." Unusual situations such as these highlight the distinction between bodily movements and action which often remains concealed in more ordinary discourse.

I have introduced this discussion of the scope of causal analysis into the essay firstly in order to support the relatively specific point that a causal account of human actions is possible which does not involve any reference to reasons (Ryle), and secondly in order to illustrate the more general point that a distinction between reasons and causes is possible. I need not enter

into discussion of criticism of the distinction --
such as Donald Davidson's famous article[32] and
the controversy provoked by it[33] -- because most
of this criticism aims at attacking the distinction from the "reasons" side. It tries to show
that a separate category of reasons, completely
independent of causal notions, does not exist.
No one to my knowledge has attacked the distinction from the other side, by showing that an independent category of causal notions does not exist,
that causal explanations can be subsumed under
those of a "reasons" or justificatory type. Only
an attack from this quarter would be relevant
to my interpretation of Hume, as I hope will be
apparent from what follows.

All the ingredients are present in Hume on
moral judgment, I believe, for an interpretation
of his thought along strictly causalist lines --
in fact of a particular kind of causal explanation, Hempel's deductive-nomological model.[34]
Let us take as an example the moral duty of gratitude, which Hume himself utilizes in his arguments
against Wollaston.[35] How does this duty arise
for Hume? First there are certain facts to be
considered, what one might describe as initial
conditions. Mr. Jones has been X's benefactor.
He has generously endowed X's entire education,
making it possible for X to achieve whatever economic or social status he has. He has now asked
a special favor of X, to serve as a tutor to his
grandchild, and advise him on his educational
needs. According to Hume, once these initial
factors are given, an almost automatic process
ensues. X feels a sentiment of approbation well
up within him at the thought of showing gratitude
towards his benefactor. An element of conscious
reflection enters for Hume in the fact that this
sentiment arises when X considers the virtue of
gratitude in a relatively disinterested fashion --
i.e., the overall benefits to be reaped from a
widespread adoption of the social practice of

showing gratitude. When X pursues this thought -- and according to Hume we are so constituted by the operation of sympathy that we cannot help entertaining this thought if we have been properly socialized and educated -- a sentiment of approval follows. This sentiment of approval supports the moral judgment that the act of gratitude in question ought to be performed.

We may now translate Hume's theory of moral judgment into the following neutral covering law schema:

Event to be explained: Y's moral judgment that X's act of gratitude should be performed.

Initial Conditions: X knows that Jones is his benefactor.

Covering Law: When Y considers disinterestedly the effects of performing the act of gratitude in question, a sentiment of approbation wells up within him; when he finds someone refraining from performing such an act of gratitude, he is overcome with disapproval.

(This law of course would apply to any human being whose vantage point was similar to Y's, since we all possess a similar capacity for sympathy.)

We are finally in a position, I believe, to grasp the true import of the "is-ought paragraph." Neither the descriptivist[36] interpretation offered by MacIntyre, nor the subjectivist interpretation advanced by Hunter, is correct. MacIntyre's interpretation is predicated on the assumption that a deductive account is ruled out, and he is chiefly preoccupied with discovering what other sorts of bridge notions between a factual statement and a moral imperative are possible for Hume. Hunter by offering a subjectivist interpretation makes it impossible for Hume to account for ethical disagreement. In contrast to both MacIntyre and Hunter, I believe that the context of Hume's thought as a whole, and the context of the chapters on moral judgment -- and the language that Hume uses -- indicate that he believes that his interpretation of moral judgment succeeds where others have failed precisely because it is a deductivist explanation of a special sort, which takes the laws of human nature into account.

Hume's argument against Wollaston, for example, is not simply that he fails to recognize the need to justify the additional premise that acts of lying are wrong. If my interpretation of Hume in Appendix I to the Second Enquiry is correct, then he wishes to level the additional argument against Wollaston that no matter what one's ultimate premise is -- whether lying is one's summum malum or something else -- one could never meet the charge of arbitrariness. Any purely justificatory account of moral judgment would have to fail because it could not meet this charge. Only a causal, deductivist account of moral judgment would remedy the deficiencies that Hume finds in the arguments of his predecessors -- that they arbitrarily take certain ends of human nature for granted, thereby falsifying the relationship between reason and the passions; that they fail to realize that a middle premise is needed linking together a statement of a particular state of affairs with the utterance of a moral judgment; that they overlook the fact that no matter what particular factual or evaluative middle premise they choose their attempt is bound to founder on the charge of arbitrariness. Only a deductivist account of moral judgment -- which deduces moral judgments from certain universal psychological laws concerning human nature -- could fill the breach created by Hume's attacks on his predecessors and contemporaries.

In the "is-ought paragraph," I believe, Hume is leveling a two-front attack against his opponents. He is making the lesser charge that some of his predecessors and contemporaries did not recognize the need for some bridge premise between a description of a particular state of affairs and the utterance of a moral judgment -- "For as this ought or ought not expresses some new relation or affirmation 'tis necessary that it should be observed and explained." Hume, however, is also making the larger claim that other philosophers have not recognized that any form of this middle premise, if couched in justificatory, non-causal language, would fail at the task of deductively explaining our moral judgments: "and at the same time that a reason should be given for what seems altogether inconceivable how this new relation can be a deduction from others, which are entirely different from it." The word "deduction" should be taken literally. It is not simply the bridge argument that is missing in his opponents, but the possibility of accounting deductively for moral judgment. It is this possibility, I believe, that Hume proposed to demonstrate in his own account.

Considering the particular constraints that Hume has placed on an adequate theory of moral argument -- his non-cognitivism and non-naturalism -- he faces an especially acute dilemma at this point in outlining his own theory of moral judgment. If the only logically proper form of moral argument is couched in the idiom of universal law, then the conclusion of such an argument can only be stated in third-person discourse: So-and-so will judge such-and-such on a particular occasion. No implication, of course, follows from this concerning the correctness of the judgment. In the logical rigor which he imposes on the proper form of moral argument, the most essential feature of such an argument -- its conclusion that a particular judgment is correct -- seems to have eluded Hume's grasp. How does Hume make the move from his discussion of the logical constraints upon moral argument to a delineation of a particular form of argument that would entail the conclusion -- "And the moral judgment is correct?" In my attempt to answer this question I shall begin with a brief summary of Hume's argument in Section Two, of Part One, of Book Three of the <u>Treatise</u> -- where Hume ostensibly presents his own theory of moral judgment. I shall then proceed to show how I think Hume's account needs to be supplemented with views advanced elsewhere in his philosophy, in order to render his positive theory of moral judgment more nearly intelligible.

2. Hume's Theory of Moral Judgment and the Doctrine of Sympathy

Hume's epistemology provides him with a limited set of alternatives. If the origin of something cannot be attributed to ideas, it must be attributed to impressions -- either external or internal. Since Hume's arguments in Section One had already disposed of the possibilities that the origin of moral judgments might be found in either ideas or external impressions, the only possibility remaining is to trace their origin to internal impressions. This establishes Hume's program in Section Two.

The classic formulation of Hume's position on moral judgment is contained in the following passage:

> An action, or sentiment, or character is virtuous or vicious; why? because its view causes a pleasure or uneasiness of a certain kind. In giving a reason therefore for the pleasure or uneasiness, we sufficiently explain the vice or virtue. To have the sense of virtue is nothing but to feel a satisfaction of a

particular kind from the contemplation of a character. The very feeling constitutes our praise or admiration. We go no farther; nor do we enquire into the cause of the satisfaction. We do not infer a character to be virtuous because it pleases: But in feeling that it pleases after such a particular manner, we in effect feel that it is virtuous. The case is the same as in our judgments concerning all kinds of beauty, and tastes and sensations. Our approbation is implied in the immediate pleasure they convey to us.[37]

The question immediately arises if the pleasure or pain that we feel concerning a particular person or event explains the origin of moral judgment, are we not faced with the same problem we encountered earlier of being able to limit moral judgments to the class of things to which we ordinarily apply them? Would not inanimate objects also come within the purview of moral judgments according to Hume's theory? Hume answers by saying that only a special kind of pleasure or pain can be regarded as supporting a moral sentiment of approbation or disapprobation. Only when the sentiment that we feel grows out of a disinterested consideration of the tendencies of particular persons or actions to promote the general welfare can our sentiment be qualified as uniquely moral.. Also, the structure of moral sentiments is such that we relate not only to their objects but to them in ways which follow the course of the four passions of pride and humility, love and hatred, and indeed in a substantive way the moral sentiments are closely linked with these four passions.

Hume now adds a caveat, in conformity with his Newtonian principles,[38] that he should not be understood as saying that as a moral scientist he is required to identify and classify the separate pleasures and pains corresponding to the different virtues and vices. Human nature, like external nature, operates with a minimum of general principles which are extremely far-reaching and multifarious in their effects. The distinction drawn by some moralists between virtue and vice -- that virtue refers to whatever is in conformity with nature and vice to whatever is unnatural -- is useless in helping us to evolve a general principle differentiating vice from virtue because of the various senses in which the word nature is used, none of which allows us to draw the distinction along recognizable lines. If one uses nature as a contrasting term with miracles, then both vice and virtue are equally natural. Where the term natural is opposed to what is unusual, vice appears as more natural than virtue. When natural is contrasted with artificial, both vice and virtue are equally artificial, since they refer to actions taken to execute a specific intent.

The general principle which elucidates the distinction between vice and virtue must therefore summarize the fact that the former are associated with painful feelings and the latter with pleasurable feelings. Partially in order to prevent this principle from deteriorating into an endless casuistry, Hume introduces the further qualification that the pleasure or pain must arise from a "general view or survey" -- that is, that it must qualify as a disinterested judgment. Hume prides himself that having framed the distinction in this way he has already achieved a good portion of what he set out to accomplish in his discussion of morals, and proceeds next with an analysis of justice and injustice.

Hume has now introduced into his analysis of moral judgment an element which does not appear to accord with the non-naturalist and

non-cognitivist strains described previously.
The class of moral judgments is delimited by a
reference to the public interest. Even though
Hume in his critique of rationalist theories of
ethics argues for an image of the relationship
between reason and the passions in which reason
plays a subservient role to the passions, when
he comes to outline his own positive theory of
moral judgment the irrationalist component seems
to become sequestered, and only those judgments
that meet an apparently rational standard of
conformity to the public interest can qualify
as moral judgments at all. The modern term, descriptivism, encapsulates, I believe, two major
tenets of moral theory to which Hume adheres and
which do not seem to cohere with his non-cognitivism and non-naturalism. The descriptivist
ethical philosopher is committed to the following
two views:

    1. It is not always logically possible to
separate the descriptive and evaluative meanings
of a moral judgment; and,

    2. The criteria applied in moral judgment
are not, in the last analysis, merely a matter
of free choice.[39]

In order to clarify the full scope of the ostensible contradictoriness of Hume's views on moral
judgment, I shall have to enter upon a discussion
of Hume's substantive ethical and political theory,
but I will postpone a more detailed analysis until
Chapter Three.

    Since Hume holds that moral injunctions are
only appropriate under certain physical and psychological conditions -- those intermediate between absolute want and absolute plenty, and complete egoism and complete benevolence[40] -- he
is predisposed towards accepting a descriptivist
account of morality. If the concept and rules

of morality arise because of the conditions of relative scarcity and limited benevolence that prevail among human beings, then the rules that human beings adopt to remedy this condition -- to alleviate some of its more rigorous severities -- will obviously fall within a certain range. Societal and individual imperatives for security and survival will both generate and delimit the range of issues to be appraised from a moral perspective.

Aside from his descriptivist account of the circumstances of justice, the role of convention in Hume's ethics can, I think, be most plausibly interpreted from a descriptivist perspective. Promise-keeping and observing the laws of property and justice have their origin for Hume in an agreement reached between human beings in whom habits of reasoning appropriate to a partially disinterested observer have already begun to be inculcated through the socializing agency of the family and the operations of sympathy. These human beings soon reach a stage of altruistic enlargement of self where they can perceive the necessity of imposing certain constraints on their behavior to remedy some of the harshness imposed by the human conditions of relative scarcity and limited benevolence. What appears to happen in Hume's scheme is that at a comparatively early stage in its development individual members of a society become capable of communicating to each other the need for the establishment of some sort of descriptivist ethics -- to determine which social institutions will accommodate best the special needs and vulnerabilities of human beings, and be most conducive to a harmonious social life.

The best way, I think, to resolve the tension in Hume's thought between his non-cognitivism and his non-naturalism and his descriptivism is to regard Hume as speaking from two perspectives. Hume in passages such as the following seems to be aware of two vantage points from which his philosophy was written. "My practice, you say, refutes my doubts. But you mistake the purport of my question. As an agent I am quite satisfied in the point; but as a philosopher who has some share of curiosity, I will not say skepticism, I want to learn the foundation of this inference."[41] "We may imagine we feel a liberty within ourselves; but a spectator can commonly infer our actions from our motives and character; and even where he cannot, he concludes in general that he might were he perfectly acquainted with every circumstance of our situation and temper, and the most secret springs of our complexion and disposition."[42] In these passages Hume draws attention to the distinction between an agent and a spectator as being relevant for an understanding of his philosophy. He appears to define the distinction as that between an ordinary unself-conscious state of mind and a reflective, philosophically curious state of mind. The chief way, I think, to make sense of the interweaving of non-cognitivist, non-naturalist and descriptivist strands in Hume's moral philosophy is to sort them out in the light of the distinction between an agent's and a spectator's perspective. The non-cognitivism and non-naturalism are advanced from the spectator's position, and the descriptivism is presented from an agent's point of view. Lest one think that human beings can simply choose whether to adopt the agent's perspective, Hume throughout Book Three, and indeed in the _Treatise_ generally, makes constant reference to the human capacity for sympathy, which suggests that there is something bizarre in trying to abstract from the perspective of sympathy altogether. Hume's discussion of sympathy would lead one to believe that the distinction between agent and spectator is not a neutral one, but a value-laden one that might more accurately be re-described as that between an inhuman, philosophical, purely logical intelligence and a more strictly human one. Hume's doctrine of sympathy appears crucial for the way he draws the agent-spectator distinction, and it is therefore to an examination of that doctrine that we must now turn.

In most cases in the Treatise where Hume employs the word "sympathy," it is being used in the sense of our capacity to recreate within ourselves another person's feelings, attitudes or states of mind, as these are conveyed to us through his outward behavior, as, for example, when Hume speaks of the idea of a sentiment or passion becoming "so inlivened (through the mechanism of sympathy) as to become the very sentiment or passion."[43] Less frequently, "sympathy" connotes for Hume the enlargement of this process of primary identification to include a wider circle of people than just our immediate family and friends, and a wider network of concerns than those in which our interests are immediately affected. In supporting the view that Hume has a dual notion of sympathy, perhaps the appropriate place to turn is to Hume's discussion of the convention establishing the rules of justice. Here our capacity for sympathy is invoked -- either openly or tacitly -- at practically every stage of the argument in Hume's elucidating how we come to see the necessity for rules of justice. Since the notion of sympathy appears here in multiple contexts in the course of a single argument, it would seem to be a good place to test its precise connotations for Hume.

In considering the question why we attach a moral obligation to the rules of justice[44] -- over and above the natural obligation which we feel in obeying them in cases where they further our individual interests -- Hume summarizes and expands upon his previous argument concerning how we come to recognize and accept the rules of justice. After men perceive the centrality of avidity, of the drive to amass as much wealth

as possible, in governing their behavior, they
gradually realize that a universal display of
avidity, unregulated by any ground rules for the
amassing and protection of wealth, would be self-
defeating. People's avid impulses would be
thwarted by aggressive interplay with the avid
impulses of others, and instead of accumulating
wealth, their very security and survival would
be threatened. In order to obviate this result,
certain ground rules for the acquisition of property -- the laws of justice -- are universally
adopted, and their rigorous enforcement is approved. The motivation to obey the rules of justice -- which require the stability of possessions, their transfer by consent, and the keeping
of promises -- is strongest in a small society,
dominated by large families and their circles
of friends, where we can sympathize with any in-
fringements of the rules of justice that might
occur. However, as geographic area and population
increase, our capacity to sympathize instinc-
tively, as it were, with violations of the rules
has a tendency to become blunted, as victim and
perpetrator are no longer immediately related
to us.

Though occasional non-observance of the rules
of justice in a large society does not produce
an immediately disruptive effect, our capacity
for sympathy itself fosters a correction mechanism
which enables us to rectify our judgments according to a more enlightened view of our interests.
The first stage in this correction process occurs,
Hume says, when we ourselves, or a member of our
immediate circle of family or friends, become
the victims of other people's acts of injustice.
We then pronounce the aggressors as unjust. The
second stage takes place when other people with
whom we are not personally familiar become the
victims of injustice. Here sympathy in what I
shall call the primary sense comes into play.
Recalling the time when we, or members of our

immediate family or friends, were victims of injustice, we project ourselves into the position of those who suffer from injustice, and condemn the aggressors from their point of view. A third stage in the enlarging of our judgments occurs when we learn to apply the disinterested judgment evolved in the second stage against ourselves, when we are tempted to perpetrate acts of injustice.

For Hume our capacity to make moral judgments where our interests are not immediately affected, such as in a large society or about a society that is remote from us in space and time, proceeds to a large extent from our rational awareness how violations of the rules of justice under such circumstances injure the fabric of society in which they take place. "Nay," Hume says, "when the injustice is so distant from us, as no way to affect our interest, it still displeases us; because we consider it as prejudicial to human society, and pernicious to every one that approaches the person guilty of it."[45] We rationally recognize -- as Hume's elaboration of the notion of convention makes clear[46] -- how any act of injustice weakens the foundations of order in society, by undermining the background of trust between the members that serves as a necessary pre-condition for their entering the convention establishing the rules of justice. It is only because each member assumes that every other member of society is rationally aware of the necessity for establishing the rules of justice that he agrees to relinquish some of his rights to make possible the institution of the rules of justice.

This rational recognition of the necessity of the rules of justice which the members of society are presumed to have -- and which encompasses remote as well as immediate violations -- is buttressed in Hume's scheme by certain non-rational propensities and capacities in man. We

are probably abetted in making our judgments about
violations of the rules of justice that occurred
in ancient Rome, for example, by the principles
of association governing our judgment. Since
we imagine the people of Rome as not being very
different from us, nor the conditions for order
in their society as differing very radically from
our own, we project the need in their society
for the same rules of justice that we recognize
as essential in our own, and condemn any violations of those rules.[47]

At the present day in our large societies
Hume invokes the mechanism of sympathy in order
to explain our capacity to make principled moral
judgments. ". . . Yet we fail not to extend it
(moral judgment) even to our own actions. The
general rule reaches beyond those instances from
which it arose; while at the same time we naturally sympathize with others in the sentiments they
entertain of us. Thus self-interest is the original motive to the establishment of justice:
but a sympathy with public interest is the source
of the moral approbation which attends that virtue."[48] "Those instances" in which the rule first
arose refers to the violations which took place
in a small society, where even if we were not
the immediate victims we could easily re-enact
within ourselves their feelings of hurt and pain.
A kind of intermediate stage on the way to our
learning how to make principled moral judgments
is reached when in a large society we consider
an "injustice (that) is so distant from us, as
no way to affect our interest." Since we are
as unrelated to the victim as we are to the aggressor, our emotions are not engaged, and we
are able to allow our rational awareness concerning the necessity of the rules of justice in pre-
serving society to predominate in our judgment.
Our rational awareness directs our capacity for
sympathy as it were at the victim rather than
at the aggressor.

The final stage in our development of fully principled moral judgments is reached "when we naturally sympathize with others in the sentiments they entertain of us." In a large society when we commit an aggressive act our rational awareness of the need for the rules of justice directs our capacity for sympathy towards the victims of our aggression, and we are thus led to condemn our own actions. The manifestation of sympathy at this level of our own involvement is in effect a transformation of primordial sympathy which was first aroused in connection with concrete individuals with whom we existed in intimate association into a more generalized, abstract capacity which focuses upon principles rather than persons. Hume has traced a continuum of the enlargement of our capacity to experience sympathetic emotion from the case in a small society where our emotions are more immediately aroused to one where strong elements of self-discipline and self-education are needed in order to channel our emotions in directions dictated by our more enduring rational concerns.

Even at the outset, however, in a small society sympathy never merely represents for Hume the outpouring of undisciplined emotion. To identify with the victim rather than the aggressor requires us to weigh even there the interests of society as a whole. It is just Hume's opinion that upon rational consideration most human beings would recognize the total coincidence between their self-interest and the interests of this larger but still imaginatively fairly easily graspable unit. Reason and emotion, foresight and imagination exist in complete mutual interdependence for Hume, reenforcing each other in the task of escaping the isolation of self and establishing connections with others by instituting an objective, common, social world. Emotion abets reason -- and rational considerations enlarge our imaginative capacity -- as we move through

Hume's three stages[49] on the way to our learning how to make principled moral judgments. The fact that a process of enlargement does take place -- so that we are able finally to articulate moral judgments from the perspective of a relatively disinterested observer -- should not obscure the fact that principled moral judgments for Hume always continue to reflect a regard for our own self-interest. Our final acquiescence even in such a bona fide moral judgment as the one we make in a large society that taking someone else's property is wrong is predicated upon the assumption that such a judgment protects our "individual interest."[50] What Hume really traces in the long paragraph on pages 498-500 of the Treatise is the education of an egoistic individual, and Stage Three of the evolutionary process that Hume describes can be labeled "principled moral judgment" only when compared with a base-line of judgments determined along excessively narrow lines.[51]

The process of virtuous circularity that I have just described between Hume's notions of rational insight and sympathy has a parallel in Hume's description of the relationship between reason and experience in a long footnote in the First Enquiry.

> There is no man so young and unexperienced as not to have formed, from observation, many general and just maxims concerning human affairs and the conduct of life; but it must be confessed that when a man comes to put these in practice, he will be extremely liable to error, till time and farther experience both enlarge these maxims, and teach him their proper use and application. In every situation or incident there are many particular and seemingly minute circumstances, which the man of greatest talent is at first apt to overlook

though on them the justness of his con
clusions and consequently the prudence
of his conduct entirely depend. Not to
mention that to a young beginner the
general observations and maxims occur
not always on the proper occasions, nor
can be immediately applied with due
calmness and distinction. The truth is
an unexperienced reasoner could be no
reasoner at all, were he absolutely unexperienced; and when we assign that
character to any one, we mean it only
in a comparative sense, and suppose him
possessed of experience, in a smaller and
more imperfect degree.^{52}

In this paragraph, Hume graphically depicts
a seamless web between reason and experience.
All reasoning, all generalization must have its
basis in experience. Yet experience itself would
remain unassimilable if we did not attempt to
delimit it through our observation of certain
regularities and our positing of various conceptual categories. Similarly, with regard to the
respective contributions of rational insight and
sympathy towards the framing of moral judgments,
Hume appears to view their relationship as forming
a seamless web. Our rational insight into the
foundations of society and our own well-being
would be impossible without an imaginative faculty
that allowed us to project ourselves into the
positions of others. Yet sympathy and imagination
themselves would not yield any insights for the
governance of our lives if these capacities were
not shaped by a certain degree of rational awareness.^{53}

Hume draws two additional parallels to the
enlargement process taking place in moral judgment: One in the broad area of communication
with others, and the other with regard to our
perception of physical objects. Concerning

communication Hume says that, "Our servant if diligent and faithful may excite stronger sentiments of love and kindness than Marcus Brutus as represented in history; but we say not upon that account that the former character is more laudable than the latter. We know that were we to approach equally near to that renowned patriot he would command a much higher degree of affection and admiration. Such corrections are common with regard to all the senses; and indeed 'twere impossible we could ever make use of language, or communicate our sentiments to one another, did we not correct the momentary appearances of things, and overlook our present situation."[54] I believe that in this passage Hume is implicitly referring to a correction process analogous to the one he describes in the case of moral judgment. We are supposed to envisage our capacity for sympathy and our rational awareness of the need to communicate with others as mutually reenforcing each other to the extent which allows us to evolve fairly stable descriptive and evaluative vocabularies. Similarly, with regard to perception, Hume says, "The case is here the same as in our judgments concerning external bodies. All objects seem to diminish by their distance: But tho' the appearance of objects to our senses be the original standard by which we judge of them, yet we do not say that they actually diminish by the distance; but correcting the appearance by reflexion, arrive at a more constant and established judgment concerning them."[55] Here too our original judgments of objects are corrected in the light of our larger rational concern over communication with others, which in turn was influenced by our sympathetic re-enactment of their predicament in not comprehending our purely subjective judgments. This imaginative capacity in turn was partially shaped by our natural concern for communication with others -- so that the interdependence between reason and imagination continues through every stage of the developmental process.

This process of what Hume would regard as virtuous circularity explains for him the origin of our making comprehensible moral, evaluative and perceptual judgments.[56]

We are now in a position to resolve the dilemma outlined above concerning Hume's intentions in the "is-ought paragraph." It appeared that in his arguments against the rationalists Hume had gone too far. The only form of argument that emerged as legitimate when all of his constraints on moral judgment were taken into account was one whose middle premise was a universal law. This meant that the conclusion of the argument would be stated in the language of indirect discourse -- "People will judge in certain ways" -- which carried no implication whatever concerning the correctness of the judgment. By the very extremism of his attack against the rationalists, Hume seemed to have landed himself in the paradoxical position of sanctioning as the only legitimate form of moral argument one in which all the steps were factual. It seemed as if the only form of moral argument that could be found acceptable was one whose conclusion was stated in nonmoral terms. We can now see, however, after our discussion of sympathy, how Hume was able to avoid this paradoxical and self-defeating result. The correctness of the judgment that the conclusion of the argument in third person discourse yields is already guaranteed in the premises of the argument. By referring to the mechanism of sympathy in his premises, the spectator is already making a covert reference to the correctness of the judgment, since what attests to its correctness for Hume is just the fact that it is motivated by sympathy.

Taken literally the language of the "is-ought paragraph" thus appears too strong. Hume does not want to say that one cannot deduce "ought" from "is" under all circumstances. You cannot deduce "ought" from "is" only if you stick strictly to statements about the world. You can, however, make this deduction if you take a detour through the psychological capacities of an agent. This detour through an agent which Hume takes is paralleled by his philosophical strategy in the case of causal judgment.57 But the detour which Hume takes is never more than that. At the conclusion of the argument, it is the authentic first person judgment which is affirmed, its rightness having already been certified by the inclusion of a premise about the operation of sympathy.

Having elucidated Hume's doctrine of sympathy, we are now also in a position to appreciate the true import of Hume's highly ambiguous statement that "The very feeling constitutes our praise or admiration."58 This phrase can mean either that when moral judgments are made certain feelings happen as a matter of fact to be present; or, that a correct moral judgment depends upon certain feelings being present. Hume's whole discussion of sympathy however -- with its connotation of a standard against which to measure people's actual moral utterances -- seems to suggest the latter interpretation of the corrected feeling serving as the basis of the judgment. Thus, in the course of outlining his own theory of moral judgment which was created to avoid the pitfalls of certain forms of rationalism and naturalism, Hume yet preserves a cognitive element which makes ethical disagreement a meaningful, and sometimes fruitful, enterprise.

Let us summarize our conclusions concerning Hume's meta-ethics. In elucidating Hume's theory of moral judgment, interpreters seem to face a logical dilemma: Is Hume not deducing the "ought" statements of moral judgment from certain psychological facts about human beings, and thus violating his own strictures against deducing an "ought" from an "is?" A central attraction of my deductivist, covering-law interpretation of Hume's account of moral judgment is that it allows us to come to grips with this objection, and to be able to discern more clearly how Hume in fact argued. If Hume's argument is construed in a scientific, law-governed, deductive sense then the charge that I have just leveled against him vanishes. His psychologism can be seen in its true perspective as a unique blending of subjective and objective elements. The actuating force behind moral judgment are certain feelings in man. These feelings, however, are not random in their behavior, nor are they the privileged possession of certain individuals. They operate uniformly throughout human nature, and are governed by universal laws which Hume believed could be empirically tested. From a knowledge of these laws, together with the presence of certain initial conditions, one can deduce that a certain moral judgment will be made. Since it is being made on the basis of sympathy, it will be for Hume the correct moral judgment. The objective factor in Hume's account of moral judgment -- which helps clarify how ethical disagreement is possible for him -- is his contention that the feelings of approval and disapproval which we experience are not to be regarded as the affective base of a moral judgment unless they are felt in response to a relatively disinterested assessment of the net good to be achieved by a particular course of action. Of this kind of disinterested assessment, we are in principle always capable. In deriving moral judgments from certain sentiments in man, Hume, in effect, reconverts a logical question -- about the permissibility of deriving "ought" from "is" -- into an empirical one. Once he believes that he has empirical evidence supporting a correlation between moral judgment and certain sentiments in man, logical considerations pose no problem because he can derive his explanandum deductively under a covering law model of explanation.

Quine in the last section of "Two Dogmas of Empiricism"[59] also argues against the erection of a so-called logical distinction -- between the analytic and the synthetic -- into a permanent barrier against any further changes in classification as our scientific knowledge advances. Quine argues that so-called permanent logical distinctions have only a pragmatic justification, which would allow us to alter them for the sake of achieving greater coherence in our total body of knowledge. I believe that some defense such as this is necessary in order to clear Hume of the charge of inconsistency described above.

On the surface it would appear that the charge of deducing an "ought" from an "is" can be leveled against Hume in his epistemology as well.[60] For example, one could argue that in making causal judgments dependent upon the presence and cultivation of certain dispositions and habits in human beings, Hume is violating his own strictures against deducing an "ought" from an "is," because individual causal judgments are made only within a framework which posits a causal category in the interpretation of experience.[61] Within this framework, one can elaborate criteria for determining which particular causal judgments are legitimate, and which are not. The framework itself, however, has merely a pragmatic justification in the explanatory power and predictability it affords us in organizing our experience. The framework itself, therefore, one could say, has a normative character which cannot be deduced from certain psychological facts about man. Hume's retort here would have to be similar to our defense of him against the charge of having violated the logical gap between "is" and "ought" in his account of moral judgment. If he can show, as he claims he can, a uniform correlation between the utterance of causal judgments and certain psychological states in man, then the logical map has to be re-drawn to accommodate the new scientific finding. We then realize that we can offer a deductive-nomological account of causal judgment, parallel to the one advanced to explain moral judgment. In Hume's way of doing philosophy, providing a pragmatic justification of causality is insufficient. One must show its basis in human psychological motivation -- how from the way human beings are constituted they cannot help reasoning in causal terms -- in order to claim to have explained causality. Hume can thus only be criticized in terms of the model of explanation he adopts -- if the articulation of his covering law is found to be inadequate, or if his explanation sketch tacitly implies certain presuppositions which cannot be defended according to his own program of explanation -- rather than by importing presuppositions foreign to his argument, and using them as a basis upon which to attack him.

3. Hume and Twentieth Century Ethical Theories

With this interpretation of Hume on moral judgment in mind, we shall better be able to understand why some version of the moral sense theory, as outlined, for instance, by C.D. Broad in his well-known article, "Some Reflections on Moral Sense Theories in Ethics"[62] cannot in all plausibility be attributed to Hume. The Moral Sense Theory in Broad's schema would seem to fit Hume's analysis of moral judgment fairly closely. Broad proposes as the correct analysis of what he calls "the trans-subjective dispositional form"[63] of the Moral Sense Theory that utterance of a favorable moral judgment means that the particular act in question would evoke a moral pro-emotion (or in the case of an unfavorable judgment, anti-emotion) in any human being who might contemplate it. Certain qualifications about an individual being normal and in a normal state would have to be added, but these do not affect the substance of my criticism of why such a formulation of Hume's position would be misleading.

On the surface, at least, the moral sense formulation of Hume's position does seem to accommodate the contradictory aspects of his theory of moral judgment. According to Broad's statement of the theory, moral judgments have reference to certain emotions. The fact, however, that the subject of these judgments is emotion does not mean that an anarchic condition prevails with respect to moral judgment. The very term moral sense connotes a uniform response on the part of people, no matter how diverse their personal histories or their current particular vantage points. The twin aspects of Hume's view on moral judgment -- its basis in emotion and its uniform expression -- seem to be accommodated in this version of the moral sense theory. Why then would it be inaccurate to attribute this theory to Hume?

The answer has to do with certain logical constraints which Hume appears to have imposed on his own argument. That an act evokes a moral pro-emotion in a human being who contemplates it is a factual statement. What provides the bridge between this statement of fact and the evaluative judgment that one ought to perform the act in question, if Hume's strictures on "is-ought" are to be taken seriously? In order to meet the constraint of "is-ought," it is best to construe Hume's argument on moral judgment as being deductive in form.[64] Hume saw himself in the role of a moral scientist who could provide a sketch for a statement of initial conditions and covering law both sufficient and necessary to deduce the required explanandum -- in this case particular moral judgments.

At which precise point the capacity for sympathy enters into the account of an individual agent's moral judgment will differ depending upon whether the judgment is viewed genetically or logically. Genetically the progression seems to be somewhat as follows: The circumstances of justice defined by a general condition of relative scarcity and limited benevolence are first ameliorated by the workings of a socialization process predicated upon the laws of associationistic psychology and by primary sympathy. The newborn child through the laws of associationism and the manifestation of primary sympathy comes to identify with the interests and needs of his immediate family, and then with a larger circle of friends. Since the laws of associationism and the presence of primary sympathy fuel the socialization process, that process can be safely extended only as far as those laws and primary sympathy reach. Since the interests and needs of the family and a small circle of friends can be more tangibly represented to the self than those of a whole society, the socialization process and primary sympathy cannot be regarded as safely extended to include identification with the imperatives of survival and growth of a whole society. The limited scope of the socialization process and primary sympathy needs to be corrected by the operation of secondary sympathy, which allows us to attain to the perspective of a relatively disinterested observer, and to frame general rules for the governance of our individual moral judgments from his perspective. As we have seen in our discussion of the cognitive element in Hume's ethical theory, only a sentiment of approbation that results from a corrected moral judgment can qualify as a true moral sentiment according to Hume. Presumably, the laws necessary for the preservation of society -- e.g., those relating to the keeping of promises and the observance of the laws of property -- would come within the purview of moral judgments corrected by the workings of secondary sympathy.

Logically, however, the circumstances of justice stand in a special relationship to sympathy. After the notion of secondary sympathy has made possible the introduction of the perspective of the relatively disinterested observer, Hume must be able to explain which facts this observer needs to know in order to form his judgments. In order to render his account of the correction mechanism at work in moral judgment free from the charge of circularity, Hume must be able to account for this knowledge without referring to disinterestedness or any other kindred term. Firth, in his article, "Ethical Absolutism and the Ideal Observer,"[65] in order to render his description of the ideal observer free from circularity makes him omniscient. In effect, he makes him know much more than he needs to know in order to offer correct moral judgments so as not to make the criteria of his knowledge dependent upon the very concept of the ideal observer which he is seeking to explain. Hume's doctrine of sympathy allows him to escape this difficulty because as we have seen according to him our capacity for primary sympathy leads us to be concerned about achieving a stable vocabulary in morals as well as in other spheres of discourse. Hume's dual notion of sympathy allows him to circumvent the logical difficulty described by Firth. Our identification with the perplexity suffered by our listeners when we use the terms in the moral vocabulary subjectively leads us to attempt to frame moral judgments from a relatively disinterested standpoint that will assure our being understood by others. For Hume it is thus the awareness of the problems that our primary capacity for sympathy confronts us with that sets the agenda so to speak of what the concepts of secondary sympathy and the relatively disinterested observer have to accomplish.

In deriving the rules of justice from the operation of sympathy in all of us, Hume faces

a special problem: According to his account of
the circumstances of justice at least one person
must disagree with everyone else concerning the
distribution of the scarce resources of society,
in order for the rules of justice determining
the allocation of those resources to become applicable. Yet, Hume's hypothesis of psychological
uniformity which posits a susceptibility to the
workings of a socialization process and the presence of sympathy in all of us would seem to obviate the necessity of justice. Having to cope
with this dilemma in Hume helps us I think to
put his notion of the socialization process and
his doctrine of sympathy into proper perspective.
Hume, after all, is an empiricist. Though the
socialization process and the capacity for sympathy tend to strengthen human psychological uniformity, one cannot take it for granted that the
socialization process and the capacity for sympathy achieve uniform results, and that all people
will tend to reason on social and political questions in the same relatively disinterested fashion.
Hume had read his Hobbes well enough to know that
the coercive arm of the state was necessary to
ensure observance by recalcitrants of those laws
that all men in their reasonable moments would
acquiesce in. Hume's hypothesis of psychological
uniformity is not meant therefore to preclude
disagreement about the ends of the state, or
about how allocation of scarce resources is to
be made. For Hume, as for Hobbes, questions of
agreement or disagreement, or observance or nonobservance of rules of justice, remain empirical,
which one's observation of human nature should
not make one too sanguine about. What the notion
of the socialization process and the doctrine
of sympathy, embodying as they do an hypothesis
of psychological uniformity, ensure is that making
judgments from the perspective of a relatively
disinterested observer is not a remote possibility
for man, but issues from our ordinary human nature
and remains entirely accessible to us. Facts --

of typical human behavior, like other facts --
will go on being as intractable as they have always been, but at least Hume applies a norm
against them which conforms to laws of human nature as he conceives them.

Hume's stress that moral judgments are addressed to permanent features or tendencies of
character rather than to individual acts can be
interpreted in the context of his doctrine of
sympathy as we have analyzed it. Since for Hume
the whole notion of a voluntary action depends
upon its being linked with settled habits and
dispositions in man,[66] moral criticism becomes
a sensible enterprise when it is addressed to
that psychological unit in man which is pivotal
for the conception of voluntariness. Not individual actions per se but the settled habits and
dispositions which go to constitute the mechanism
of sympathy become for Hume the proper focus of
moral criticism.

It is important to guard against a highly
sophisticated misinterpretation of Hume's ethical
theory which might result from not taking his
doctrine of sympathy sufficiently into account.
Broad, in his chapter on Hume in <u>Five Types of
Ethical Theory</u>,[67] does not seem to me to take
into account the cognitive element in Hume's
theory of moral judgment. Broad says that, according to Hume,

> Every dispute on questions of right and
> wrong is capable of being settled completely by the simple method of collecting statistics. Suppose that A thinks
> that X is right, and B thinks that X is
> wrong. We have first to make sure that
> A and B agree as to the non-ethical facts
> about X, i.e., as to its non-ethical
> qualities and relations to other things,
> as to what effects it will have and

what effects other things which might have been substituted for it would have had, and so on. Suppose that when all differences and confusions on these nonethical matters have been removed, A still thinks that X is right and B still thinks that X is wrong. If Hume's theory be true this means that A thinks that most men would feel an emotion of approval on contemplating X, while B thinks that most men would feel an emotion of disapproval on contemplating X. Now this is a question which can be settled by experiment, observation, collection of statistics and empirical generalization. This seems to me simply incredible.[68]

This interpretation seems to overlook entirely the cognitive element in Hume's theory of moral judgment. Hume offers a kind of paradigm case argument as to how a properly constituted individual -- one whose mechanism of sympathy is functioning intact -- will judge. Broad attributes to Hume the view that moral judgments are simply sociological reports as to how people will in fact judge. Hume, however, never says this. What other people think, considered in isolation from what it is proper for them to think, does not form part of the cognitive part of the judgment for Hume. On Broad's view, Hume is simply bereft of any plausible account of ethical disagreement, whereas in fact Hume has a quite cogent theory of ethical disagreement.

Ethical disagreement, for Hume, does not revolve around the question about what people do in fact decide, but rather about what they should decide. However, since what people should decide is relatively fixed by the perspective of what accords with the general rules of moral judgment -- examples of which Hume provides in

51

his chapters on property and justice -- ethical disagreement is usually reduced to the search for strategies in making the recalcitrant party or parties live up to their full human potential. Hume offers no panaceas or short-cuts here, but points to the necessity of socialization and education in order to nurture the other-regarding virtues and capacities in man. In ethical disagreement, we, or, a third party, as the case might be, try to educate or reeducate our opponent to that perspective from which it would be possible for him to formulate general rules, and to criticize his behavior and judgments accordingly.

In order to get Hume's ethical theory as a whole most sharply into focus, it might be useful to compare it with modern ethical doctrines that borrow from it and differ from it in a variety of ways -- emotivism, prescriptivism and descriptivism. I shall discuss them in this order, devoting my major attention to the contrast with emotivism, because its debt to Hume appears to be the largest, and where the two differ, we might gain additional insight into the motivation behind Hume's ethical theory.

In his classic essay, "The Emotive Meaning of Ethical Terms,"[69] Stevenson lays down the following three constraints on any adequate philosophical theory of ethics:

1. Contrary to what have been called interest theories in ethics, which define goodness in terms of such psychological attitudes as approval or desire, Stevenson stresses that an adequate ethical theory must explain how goodness might be a topic for ethical disagreement. According to the interest theories, ethical disagreement is ruled out. Since "this is good" might be translated for example as, "I desire this," ethical disagreement becomes impossible

because one's opponent in arguing against the thesis that the object is good is simply saying that he does not desire it which does not contradict the first speaker's statement.

2. An adequate ethical theory must be able to account for the feelings of attraction or revulsion towards certain types of action that ethical judgments express on the part of a speaker and are intended to evoke from his listeners. Stevenson terms these emotional concomittances of ethical judgments, "the magnetism of ethical terms."

3. Stevenson adds a third constraint on any adequate ethical theory which is again mainly directed against interest theories in ethics. According to the interest theories, the goodness of anything could be verified solely by uses of the scientific method. If a person for example could scientifically establish that he was not in error about his desires, he would have proven his ethical judgments. The autonomy of ethics is denied on this view, as the study of ethical judgments becomes a branch of the science of psychology. A second argument which Stevenson adduces against the view that the meaning of ethical terms could be discovered solely through the scientific method is that it cannot meet G.E. Moore's famous open question objection. "No matter what set of scientifically knowable properties a thing may have, you will find on careful introspection that it is an open question to ask whether anything having these properties is good."[70]

Stevenson rejects those positions in ethics which we have seen Hume also finds unacceptable for reasons that are not dissimilar from Hume's. Rationalism, for example, is rejected by Stevenson because it fails to meet his second restraint -- i.e., it cannot account for the magnetism of ethical judgments. Subjectivism is attacked because it cannot explain ethical disagreement.

Considering that many of their targets are the same, the answer to the question whether Stevenson will align himself with Hume's position in ethics will depend upon whether Stevenson joins Hume in envisioning some alternative -- outside of rationalism -- to an irreducible ethical diversity. Apparently, Stevenson is not able to visualize such an alternative because his emotive theory of meaning is intended to explain just the irreconcilable diversity of ethical judgment. Hume, by contrast, while rejecting rationalist theories in ethics still maintains that uniformity of judgment can be purchased under the aegis of science, which establishes correlations between particular ethical judgments and the internal states of an agent.

Let us now turn and examine more specifically Hume's stand on the three constraints which Stevenson imposes on any adequate ethical theory:

1. According to Stevenson, when I say that something is good I do not designate or report about certain favorable feelings in me towards a particular course of action or state of affairs. In making the statement, I express my feelings of approval about the course of action or state of affairs, and consequently when someone else expresses feelings contrary to mine towards the same object we are disagreeing in attitude. If in saying that something were good, however, I were merely designating my feelings, no disagreement would be possible between me and another person who pointed to directly contrary feelings within himself towards the same object. I could agree that the next person experienced feelings contrary to my own about a particular object, and he could agree to the same about me, and our ethical disagreement would never get off the ground, as it were. In saying that ethical statements express feelings, disagreement becomes possible. However, disagreement does not end for

Stevenson with mere expression of contrary feelings. Stevenson accepts Hume's account about the relation of reason and the passions, and consequently assign to reason a large, if ultimately subservient, role in the elaboration and settling of ethical disputes.[71] When my emotions move me towards a certain object, reason can help clarify which ends will most nearly satisfy my emotions, and it can help illuminate the means that will be most conducive towards attaining those ends. Disagreements in belief concerning certain factual states of affairs therefore mediate between differences in attitude. After a brute expression of disagreement in attitude, ethical disagreement continues between two parties when they each try to rectify each other's beliefs concerning the compatibility of the ends chosen with their professed expressions of attitude, and of the suitability of the means adopted to attain those ends.

There is an objectivist core in Hume's ethics which is lacking in Stevenson's account. Hume's deductive-nomological explanation of ethical judgment does not allow for large variation in human ethical response. His account makes it possible to predict from an adequate knowledge of background and initial conditions, and the relevant covering law(s), which ethical judgment should be forthcoming in a particular situation. The explanandum in Hume's deductive-nomological account serves as a kind of accessible norm, indicating which particular ethical judgment would be appropriate under the circumstances. In his chapters on substantive ethics, Hume underscores the elaborate socialization process and the workings of sympathy that are required before the sentiments can be regarded as properly educated to respond in the appropriate way. Thus the major focus of ethical disagreement for Hume would be to remedy the incompleteness of an opponent's moral education, when through sheer lack of thorough socialization or occasional deviance from what one would otherwise recognize as the norm, one does not utter the moral judgment that Hume's deductive-nomological account indicates to be appropriate under the circumstances. Outside of this context of rectification according to an objective standard, moral disagreement would appear to have no place in the scheme of Hume's ethics.

  2. Stevenson is able to explain the magnetism of ethical terms by identifying a special use of language which he calls emotive. Certain words in a language -- or certain usages of particular words which can be used in a descriptive way as well -- become associated preeminently with the expression of certain emotions on the part of a speaker and the simultaneous generating of corresponding emotions in a listener. The range of emotions which a word expresses, since it tends to become relatively stable over time, can then be construed as part of the meaning of that word. Stevenson here adopts a causal theory of meaning, since he identifies meaning with those psychological causes and effects which a word has a tendency to become connected with. In ethical discourse, the word "good" is used primarily in an emotive sense to indicate approval of a specific course of action, say, on the part of the speaker, and to suggest a similar feeling of approval to the listener. Thus, there can exist no "open question" when the term "good" is employed by a speaker, to the effect that once he presents his reasons for acting the way he does one can still question whether the particular course of action is good. The gap between obligation and motivation is closed by the emotive use of the term good, which links the usage of this word to the experiencing of certain favorable attitudes on the part of the speaker and the simultaneous attempt to evoke similar attitudes on the part of the listener.

Aiken, in his book Reason and Conduct,[72] offered a cogent criticism of Stevenson's theory of emotive meaning to which Hume's scientific account of ethics is not vulnerable. Stevenson had argued that in order to account for the magnetic force of ethical language he had to introduce the notion of emotive meaning as a stratum separate from descriptive meaning. Aiken, however, maintains that this violates a kind of principle of theoretical parsimony, since it is entirely possible that the emotive significance of ethical terms is mediated through its descriptive meaning. Stevenson could legitimately introduce the notion of emotive meaning only if he could show, what he has in fact failed to prove, that some propositions have a merely emotive significance and that ethical judgments conform to this type. Stevenson by postulating the notion of emotive meaning thus seems to be introducing a needless theoretical construct to account for facts that might be explained more simply.

For Hume, the magnetism of ethical terms can be scientifically explained. Once initial conditions are taken into account, one can invoke a covering law which will explain which emotions would be appropriate under the circumstances. From an enumeration of background and initial conditions and covering law together, the proper moral judgment can be deduced. In answer to the question how the word good is used dynamically -- to indicate a preference for a particular course of action on the part of a speaker and to foster the same preferences in the listener -- Hume would say that the utterance of a favorable moral judgment depends upon the person uttering the judgment experiencing certain feelings of pleasure, which are shared by his listeners. The presence of these feelings of pleasure in turn can be explained by a covering law once the initial conditions of the judgment are understood.

Striking affinities emerge between Stevenson's and Hume's accounts of the magnetism of ethical terms. Stevenson seems to have provided a correlative account in terms of a theory of meaning for Hume's scientific account of moral judgment. For, after all, what does a scientific account seek to achieve? One of its features is what one might describe as irreducibility -- the halting of the ever-widening request for explanation at the most rational stopping-place. Stevenson, for reasons which we shall go into in a moment, was unable to accept Hume's scientific account of moral judgment. He sought, however, for an analogue in the theory of meaning to the irreducibility feature which Hume's scientific account was able to provide. He found it in his emotive theory of language, which by identifying a special emotive use of language -- a use especially geared to the expressing and influencing of emotion -- could manifest irreducibility in a way analogous to Hume's scientific account. For Stevenson's schema of the relation between reason and the emotions is identical with Hume's, so that referring to an emotion means invoking an "original existence" which in an important sense can be neither rationally qualified nor explained. Stevenson sought to show that the link between moral judgment and motivation could be established at the level of a theory of meaning in a way analogous to that achieved by Hume in his scientific account of moral judgment.

Stevenson, I believe, was premature in his dismissal of all versions of moral sense theories in ethics -- as well as those theories which seek to correlate moral judgments with feelings, on the grounds that they were too subjectivistic. Stevenson rejected these theories on the grounds that they failed to meet the first constraint outlined above -- i.e., they could not account for ethical disagreement. Had Stevenson been aware of a certain subtlety in Hume's argument he would have realized that at least one version of ethical theories that correlate moral judgments with feelings could be reconstructed to account for ethical disagreement. Ethical disagreement becomes possible according to Hume's theory because of the role that sympathy plays in establishing a kind of paradigm case argument concerning how people should judge. Had Stevenson been aware of this element in Hume's ethical theory perhaps he would not have sought through an emotive theory of language for a way of accounting for ethical disagreement that could just as easily have been provided at the level of human feelings themselves construed the way Hume understands them.

3. We are now in a better position to understand Stevenson's third constraint on an adequate theory of moral judgment: Criteria of goodness must not be discovered solely through the scientific method. If scientific method could resolve ethical disagreement, there would be no room for an emotive use of language, since disagreements in attitude could always in principle be resolved into disagreements in belief. Since Stevenson adopts Hume's schema differentiating the respective spheres of reason and emotion, he imposes the additional constraint on a theory of moral judgment that its criteria of goodness not be reducible to the reasons offered on behalf of a particular moral judgment.[73] At most the reasons adduced in support of a moral judgment bear a causal relation to the judgment, while neither entailing it nor being entailed by it. For Hume, the account of moral judgment as a whole is scientific, and the observer need not adduce any reasons, scientific or otherwise, in order to explain a particular moral utterance of an agent.

Stevenson, in a sense, stands midway between Hume and Hare's prescriptivism.[74] There is

subjectivism in Stevenson -- exemplified by the
stress on the role of differences in attitude
in ethical disagreement -- but much less arbitrariness than in Hare. The emotions that undergird
ethical differences are something which we cannot
fully control rationally, so that in this sense
they are not arbitrary. Hare, on the other hand,
isolates a logical component of personal decision-making in the framing of moral judgments, which
is arbitrary. (One simply decides, for example,
according to Hare's schema, to be against flogging.) Stevenson relativizes Hume's stress on
the constancy of emotion which accompanies moral
judgment, thus introducing a subjective element,
while retaining the element of non-arbitrariness.
Hare by isolating the logical feature of personal
decision-making in moral judgment removes the
non-arbitrariness, and thus moves even further
away from Hume.

When we come to descriptivism, we are dealing
with one component of Hume's ethical theory itself,
so that whatever contrasts one might point to
between descriptivism as a substantive ethical
doctrine and Hume's meta-ethics are, so to speak,
internal to Hume's thought itself. (We shall
deal with the relationship between Hume's meta-ethics and the meta-ethics underpinning descriptivism in the summary to this section of the chapter.)[75] In dealing with descriptivism here, it
might be useful, therefore, to indicate again the
novelty of the appearance of descriptivism within
the context of Hume's ethical thought, and then
to try and show the extent, if any, to which Hume
diverges from Twentieth Century descriptivism.

There appears to be a tension in Hume's
thought between an acknowledgment of limitless
diversity in human types, aspirations and the
choices of ends of action, and an attempt to show
that in practice the range of choice is limited
by considerations that are common to all of

humanity. Hume's stress on the role of emotion in determining the ends of action would seem to indicate a limitless diversity in the range of human choice. Followers of a rationalist or natural law tradition in ethics,[76] in stressing the primacy of reason, appear to be arguing for a hierarchy of ends of action that should be universally accepted. In arguing against these traditions, Hume seems intent on destroying the notion of a hierarchy of ends. Yet, when he outlines his own schema of the emotions and assigns primacy to pain and pleasure -- it becomes clear that feelings of pleasure correlate with whatever policies or choices of action further a relatively egoistic conception of the public good, and that feelings of pain correlate with whatever choices would be detrimental to that good. Hume achieves through his picture of the workings of the emotions a result that his undermining of the traditional role of reason would appear to have obviated.

In defending a descriptivist position, Warnock, in The Object of Morality,[77] introduces a distinction which it appears to me Hume's moral philosophy stands in need of, and which conforms to the tenor of his thought. In response to the relativist attack against descriptivism, Warnock says that in order for moral judgments to apply to human beings they must conform to certain minimum standards of rationality -- "They must be able to achieve some understanding of the situations in which they are placed, to envisage alternative courses of action in those situations, to grasp and weigh considerations for or against those alternatives, and to act accordingly."[78] Presumably, a minimal observance of those requirements is uniform enough to cover the most diverse periods and circumstances. Yet, though moral principles would appear then to be universally applicable, one obviously would not want to say that moral blame should be apportioned without taking further account of the whole gamut of possible variation in individual circumstances -- viz., excuses, varying capability of moral learning, the distinction between children and adults, etc.[79] In the making of moral judgments, we appear to be in need of two sets of principles -- one for judging whether an action is right or wrong, and the other for judging whether doing the action is a sign of a bad character or not. The need for invoking a dual set of principles is also apparent in Hume. Since, according to Hume, the mechanism of approbation and disapprobation is universal, if one took only that factor into account one could not justify subtle gradations in the leveling of moral blame. Since the internal mechanism which gives rise to moral distinctions is universal, without introducing some such distinction as that between whether an action is right or wrong and whether doing it is a sign of a bad character or not one could not explain the variation in judgment that marks human moral discourse. By making such a distinction, one can then go on to say that for Hume the mere presence in human beings of the moral sentiments indicates that the first distinction is applicable to them, but that moral judgments of praise or blame must await the further determination of whether a particular action performed is a sign of a bad character or not.

A second point of interest in considering the descriptivist component of Hume's ethical theory is that Twentieth Century descriptivism, of the kind espoused by Warnock, possesses no theoretical reserves to cope with wholesale changes in people's outlook -- when, for example, the very concept and value to be assigned to rationality change. Since the time Freud wrote, the meaning of rationality has been modified by the appearance of a new term to which it is opposed -- repression. Whenever we act rationally, according to Freud, it is always at the cost of

damming up certain anarchic impulses which crave
immediate outlet. Suppose, as many people believe
has already happened, that this picture of mental
life begins to pervade the general consciousness,
and a widespread devaluation of reason -- and
the offering of specific reasons to buttress one's
actions -- takes place. How does Warnock deal
with a popular disinclination to speak the language of reasons at all?

    Before answering this question let us con-
sider another possibility which poses a challenge
to descriptivism. Suppose, as one can find among
certain avant-garde writers, that the whole scheme
which assigns pleasure a positive value and suffering or pain a negative value collapses.[80] In
the so-called Theatre of Cruelty of Artaud and
others, for example, suffering assumes an independent aesthetic value. Suppose that the values
that underpin the Theatre of Cruelty become dis-
seminated throughout a culture, and form the basis
upon which it articulates its value judgments.
How would a descriptivist respond? Warnock, at
least, counters such possibilities by invoking
what one might describe as an ultimate contingent
fact -- that a substantial proportion of human
beings do want to go on using the old terms such
as reason, reasons, pleasure and pain in much
the same sense as before. As long as these people
retain their ascendancy, however precariously,
the range of legitimate moral response will be
restricted by the meaning of some of the key terms
in the moral vocabulary.[81] Hume, I think, possesses a last bastion of theory to protect him
against this onslaught of historically relativized
fact. He can point to those internal sentiments
which according to psychological laws that he
regards as universally valid signify an approving
moral judgment when we experience pleasure, and
betoken a disapproving moral judgment when we
experience pain. In the end, however, I believe
that Hume is in no better position than Warnock,

because his psychological laws were not presented a priori, but are offered in the guise of empirical hypotheses, which later developments -- either historical or scientific -- can falsify.[82]

To summarize Hume's relationship to contemporary movements in moral philosophy, it might be useful to elaborate a schema in order to pinpoint specifically where Hume stands:

| Hume's Scientific Ethics | Emotivism & Prescriptivism | Descriptivism |

The two extremes in this schema follow diametrically opposed paradigms in doing moral philosophy. Hume follows a vindicationist paradigm in accounting for moral judgment. He vindicates our practice by showing how it is rooted in our psychology and the aims we have in view. The validationist on the other hand merely validates individual judgments. The vindicationist would argue against him that first principles according to the validationist scheme always remain arbitrary. The only way of avoiding this arbitrariness, a vindicationist would claim, is by showing how these first principles are rooted in human nature and the natural ends of man, such as security and survival. To this challenge, a modern validationist like Urmson responds that, if we compare, for example, the argument "Mr. Justice Blackstone is a good judge because he is impartial" with the argument "Mr. Justice Blackstone is a good judge because he was born on the ninth day of August," we can recognize prima facie -- without having to resort to any intervening premise about human nature, or to identify a special emotive use of language, or a class of "persuasive definitions" -- that the former is a valid moral argument, while the latter is not. Since it is always an open matter what one brings into the argument as premises, "where the criteria are well known and undisputed, there is no reason why we should not treat them rather as principles of the argument."[84]

Emotivism and prescriptivism stand in the middle with respect to the question of which paradigm they follow in delineating the prototype of legitimate moral argument. In a sense they are haunted by Hume's vindicationism, because a prime problem that they have each set for themselves is how to rescue the logical structure of moral argument once Hume's image of the relationship between reason and emotion, and his strictures against deriving an "ought" from an "is," are taken into account. The kinds of moral argument that both emotivism and prescriptivism exclude bear the marks of following a vindicationist paradigm in doing moral philosophy. However, the form of moral argument that both schools finally settle upon as legitimate enshrine either subjectivism or arbitrariness as a necessary feature of all types of moral argument, which is foreign to Hume's way of thought. Stevenson, as we saw earlier, sought to find an analogue in a theory of language to the non-arbitrariness which is so prominent a characteristic of Hume's moral philosophy. Stevenson claimed to have found it in his theory of the emotive meaning of ethical terms, which in a sense preserved the non-arbitrariness but only at the cost of introducing subjectivity into ethical argument. Hare, as we have seen, moves further away from Hume's original intentions than Stevenson. Prescriptivism introduces a kind of horizontal variant to Hume's infinite regress argument. Instead of saying that no matter what grounds one offered for a particular moral position one could still go on probing "Why?" ad infinitum, Hare's horizontal variant of this argument states that no matter what position in ethics one chose to defend, as long as he were consistent in his position -- in Hare's language, willing to universalize his argument -- it could be open to no logical objection.[85] Thus, Hare, in moving away from Stevenson, also moved even further away from Hume.

Returning to our schema, as we move from right to left the rigor of what is required in order to account for moral judgment increases. For descriptivism, no special feature or use of language needs to be identified in order to explain moral judgment. The way to identify moral discourse is simply by its subject matter, whatever subjects people have come over time to discuss from a moral perspective, i.e., whatever subjects they have come to attach paramount, or, perhaps, overriding, importance to. No hard and fast distinction can be drawn between descriptive and evaluative levels of discourse, so that one may "cordon off" a class of purely evaluative terms which form the special province of study for the moral philosopher. Any of the five general types of "illocutionary forces" identified by Austin can be used in a moral context.[86] Emotivism and prescriptivism, on the other hand, require that a special use of language be identified -- either emotive or prescriptive -- in order to explain moral judgment. Hume, however, puts the most rigorous constraint of all on the adequacy of an explanatory account of moral judgment, by requiring that certain sentiments in man be identified and correlated with the utterance of specific moral judgments.

Hume has more in common with his opponents occupying the other end of the spectrum -- the descriptivists -- than he does with those occupying the middle position, the emotivists and prescriptivists. Both the descriptivists and Hume have elaborated accounts of moral judgment which limit the degree of arbitrariness involved. For the descriptivists, the number of choices open to someone using the word "good" are not limitless. What constitutes the good for man falls within a circumscribed range. One cannot decide for himself in all cases what falls within it, and what might be excluded. For Hume, also, the degree of arbitrariness possible in the framing of moral judgments is restricted by the objects that will actuate the moral sentiments of pleasure and pain, approval and disapproval. Only a relatively disinterested assessment as to what will contribute to the general welfare, or disturb it, will arouse the proper moral sentiment, and consequently evoke the proper moral judgment, in man.

We shall now have to consider how illuminating the pattern of argument which we have discerned in Hume's ethics is in helping us unravel perplexities in his chapters on causal judgment, and in his political theory.

Footnotes

PRELIMINARY REMARKS

[1] David Hume, A Treatise of Human Nature (Selby-Bigge ed.; Oxford: Clarendon Press), pp. xix-xx. All future references to the Treatise will be to this edition.

CHAPTER I

[2] Ibid., pp. 469-470.

[3] Leslie Stephen, History of English Thought in the Eighteenth Century, Volume Two, Harbinger Books (N.Y.: Harcourt, Brace and World, 1962), pp. 1-2.

[4] Treatise, p. 413.

[5] Amelie Oksenberg Rorty, "Naturalism, Paradigms and Ideology," The Review of Metaphysics, Vol. 24 (June, 1971), p. 640.

[6] Treatise, pp. 461-462.

⁷Ibid., pp. 408-409.

⁸Amelie Rorty, op. cit.

⁹Charles L. Stevenson, *Ethics and Language*, Yale Paperbounds (New Haven: Yale University Press, 1965), pp. 81-111.

¹⁰Amelie Rorty, op. cit.

¹¹*Treatise*, pp. 469-470.

¹²See, for example, Rorty, op. cit.

¹³*Treatise*, pp. 468-469.

¹⁴What mainly motivates some at least of Hume's modern interpreters to offer a revised reading of the "is-ought paragraph" are not just Hume's derivation of moral judgments from the presence of feelings of pleasure and pain in man, but from particular kinds of pleasurable and painful feelings -- those which a relatively disinterested observer would experience in surveying man's situation with regard to his fellows. I offer an account of the sorts of feelings that are central to Hume below, pp. 30-32.

¹⁵Included in W.D. Hudson, ed., *The Is/Ought Question*, Papermac Series (London: Macmillan, 1969), pp. 35-51.

¹⁶Geoffrey Hunter, "Hume on Is and Ought," included in Hudson, op. cit., pp. 59-64.

¹⁷Ibid., pp. 62-63.

¹⁸David Hume, *Enquiries Concerning the Human Understanding and Concerning the Principles of Morals* (Second Edition; Selby-Bigge; Oxford: Clarendon Press), p. 173. All future references to the *Enquiries* will be to this edition.

[19] Ibid., p. 293.

[20] Treatise, pp. 173-176.

[21] In the discussion that follows, I am greatly indebted to Alasdair MacIntyre's article, "The Antecedents of Action," contained in Bernard Williams and Alan Montefiore, editors, British Analytical Philosophy (London: Routledge and Kegan Paul, 1967), pp. 205-226.

[22] Thomas Hobbes, Leviathan, Michael Oakeshott, editor (Oxford: Blackwell, 1946), p. 6.

[23] Treatise, p. 399.

[24] Immanuel Kant, Fundamental Principles of the Metaphysics of Ethics, Chapter Two.

[25] Gilbert Ryle, The Concept of Mind (London: Hutchinson, 1949).

[26] Ibid., pp. 65-66.

[27] Ibid., p. 64.

[28] Ibid., pp. 69-74.

[29] Ibid., p. 64.

[30] A.I. Melden, Free Action (London: Routledge and Kegan Paul, 1965), pp. 208-210.

[31] As represented for example by R.S. Peters and H. Tajfel in their article, "Hobbes and Hull: Metaphysicians of Behavior" contained in Maurice Cranston and Richard S. Peters, editors, Hobbes and Rousseau, Anchor Books (Garden City: Doubleday and Co., 1972), pp. 165-183; and G.E.M. Anscombe in her book, Intention (Oxford: Blackwell, 1957).

[32] Donald Davidson, "Actions, Reasons and Causes," reprinted in Alan R. White, editor, The Philosophy of Action (Oxford: Oxford University Press, 1968), pp. 79-94.

[33] E.g., Kurt Baier, "Reasons for Doing Something," Journal of Philosophy, LXI (1964), pp. 198-203; Daniel Bennet, "Action, Reason and Purpose," Journal of Philosophy, LXII (1965), pp. 85-96; D.W. Hamlyn, "Causality and Human Behavior," Proceedings of the Aristotelian Society, Suppl. XXXVIII (1964), pp. 125-142.

[34] Carl G. Hempel, "The Function of General Laws in History," and "Aspects of Scientific Explanation," in Hempel's Aspects of Scientific Explanation (N.Y.: The Free Press, 1965), pp. 231-244; 331-496.

[35] Treatise, pp. 461-462.

[36] For the sense in which I am using "descriptivism" see below, p. 30.

[37] Treatise, p. 471.

[38] For a fuller discussion of Hume's Newtonian principles, see below, pp. 173-175.

[39] W.D. Hudson, Modern Moral Philosophy, Anchor Books (Garden City: Doubleday and Co., 1970), p. 295.

[40] Treatise, pp. 484-488.

[41] Enquiries, p. 38.

[42] Treatise, pp. 408-409.

[43] Ibid., p. 319.

[44] Treatise, pp. 498-500.

[45] *Treatise*, p. 499.

[46] See below, pp. 126-130.

[47] In saying that a mechanism of association is involved in the moral judgments that we render about ancient Rome, I do not wish to exclude the role that sympathy also plays in Hume's view in the making of such judgments. Hume probably envisaged the relationship between them along the following lines. The laws of association create the setting as it were -- by establishing a sufficient basis of resemblance between the ancient Romans and ourselves -- for our capacity of sympathy to function.

[48] *Treatise*, pp. 499-500.

[49] If one includes in this scheme what I have earlier (p. 34) called "instinctive sympathy," then there would in reality be four stages rather than three. "Instinctive sympathy" would signify for Hume the stage where rational considerations are least prominent in directing our feelings of sympathy towards their object. However, since for Hume "instinctive sympathy" shades off beyond the smallest social unit into what I have called "primary sympathy" -- and the whole process of the evolution of sympathy represents a continuum for him, so that a rational component is present even in the earliest manifestations of sympathy -- I have for the sake of simplicity chosen to speak in the chapter only of primary and secondary sympathy as the authentic foci of Hume's concern.

[50] *Treatise*, p. 496.

[51] In a Kantian framework, for example, Hume's principled judgments might provide the starting-point which a person would have to overcome in order to be recognized as fully moral.

[52] *Enquiries*, pp. 43-45.

[53] The implications of this image of a seamless web of reason and experience, and between rational insight and sympathy, for political conservatism will be explored more fully in Chapter Three, in my discussion of Hume's theory of revolution.

[54] *Treatise*, p. 582.

[55] *Ibid.*, p. 603.

[56] I agree with David Macnabb, in his book *David Hume: His Theory of Knowledge and Morality* (Second Edition; Oxford: Blackwell, 1966), pp. 185-191, that the doctrine of sympathy presented in the *Second Enquiry* assumes a more altruistic capacity in man than does the doctrine of sympathy contained in the *Treatise*. Nevertheless, in the *Enquiries* Hume does not appear to have worked out the implications of his altered doctrine in ways that would substantially affect his views on justice, property, political obligation and causality as presented in the *Treatise*. In all these other areas Hume's views remain fundamentally unchanged from the *Treatise* to the *Enquiries*.

[57] See below, pp. 90-92.

[58] *Treatise*, p. 471.

[59] W.V.O. Quine, "Two Dogmas of Empiricism," in *From A Logical Point of View*, Harper Torchbook (New York: Harper and Row, 1963), pp. 42-46.

[60] See below, pp. 97-98, where I discuss this question in further detail.

[61] That this is true for Hume, and not merely for Kant, is argued for below,

[62] C.D. Broad, "Some Reflections on Moral-Sense Theories in Ethics," in Wilfrid Sellars and John Hospers, editors, *Readings in Ethical Theory* (First Edition; New York: Appleton-Century-Crofts, 1952), pp. 363-390.

[63] *Ibid.*, p. 365.

[64] This is not to deny that Hume's primary opponents, the ethical rationalists, could also spell out their arguments so that they would be deductive in form. What happens, though, when the rationalists unravel their arguments so that they are no longer enthymemes but fully worked out deductive arguments is that the additional premises they will have interposed between the initial premise and the conclusion will all be of a noticeably moral character. Hume claims that the rationalists would not be able to make their arguments without introducing such additional moral premises. In opposition to the rationalists, Hume tries to show how a deductive argument is possible in moral judgment by taking an "indirect loop" through the psychological capacities of an agent, without jeopardizing the strictly moral conclusions of the argument.

[65] Roderick Firth, "Ethical Absolutism and the Ideal Observer," in Wilfrid Sellars and John Hospers, editors, *Readings in Ethical Theory* (Second Edition; New York: Appleton-Century-Crofts, 1970), pp. 200-221.

[66] *Treatise*, pp. 407-409, and *passim*.

[67] C.D. Broad, *Five Types of Ethical Theory* (London: Routledge and Kegan Paul, 1970), Chapter Four.

[68] *Ibid.*, p. 115.

[69] Charles L. Stevenson, "The Emotive Meaning of Ethical Terms," in Sellars and Hospers, Second Edition, op. cit., pp. 254-266.

[70] Ibid., pp. 256-257.

[71] Charles L. Stevenson, "The Emotive Conception of Ethics and its Cognitive Implications," in Sellars and Hospers, Second Edition, op. cit., pp. 267-275.

[72] Henry David Aiken, Reason and Conduct: New Bearings in Moral Philosophy (New York: Alfred A. Knopf, 1962), pp. 62-63; 124-125, and passim.

[73] Charles L. Stevenson, "The Emotive Conception of Ethics and its Cognitive Implications," in Sellars and Hospers, op. cit.

[74] R.M. Hare's prescriptivist ethical theory is presented in The Language of Morals (Oxford: Clarendon Press, 1952); and Freedom and Reason (Oxford: Clarendon Press, 1963).

[75] See below, pp. 66-67.

[76] Here I am referring to Hume's rationalist predecessors and contemporaries whom he attacked, and not to successors like Kant who can also be regarded as rationalist or quasi-rationalist.

[77] G.J. Warnock, The Object of Morality (London: Methuen and Co., 1971).

[78] Ibid., p. 144.

[79] Ibid., pp. 145-146.

[80] In this connection, see Lionel Trilling's interesting essay, "The Fate of Pleasure: Wordsworth to Dostoevsky," in Northrop Frye, editor,

Romanticism Reconsidered (New York: Columbia University Press, 1968), pp. 73-106.

[81] Warnock, op. cit., pp. 165-166.

[82] Against the challenge to rationality which I describe in the paragraph, Kant would fare much better than Hume. What the Kantian transcendental deduction of the notion of rational agency shows is how much of our ordinary modes of discourse would have to be discarded with the abandoning of the notion of rational agency. In response to the Freudian rejection of the idea of rationality, Kantians would point to all the places in our language where people talk about their actions -- all the references to the self as agent -- which would be rendered meaningless if the concept of rationality were rejected. One might adopt an intermediate position by accepting the basic notion of rational deliberation and yet saying that it is much less efficacious in action than was once thought. The notion of rational action, however, would seem to have a hold on us to the extent that we regard ourselves as agents, rather than merely "arenas."

Hume counters the Freudian challenge, head to head, so to speak, by having a different psychology which lays great stress on a conscious theory of motivation. If his psychology should prove outmoded, he remains more exposed than Kant, who has the kind of a priori response described above.

[83] The terminology of validationism and vindicationism are derived from Herbert Feigl, "Validation and Vindication: An Analysis of the Nature and the Limits of Ethical Arguments," in Sellars and Hospers, First Edition, op. cit., pp. 667-680. However, I draw the distinction differently from Feigl. See especially pp. 674-676.

[84] J.O. Urmson, The Emotive Theory of Ethics, Galaxy Books (New York: Oxford University Press, 1968), pp. 86-87.

[85] R.M. Hare, Freedom and Reason, op. cit., p. 4.

[86] Warnock, op. cit., p. 135.

CHAPTER TWO

CAUSAL JUDGMENT

1. Noncognitivism in Causal Judgment

In his chapters on causal judgment in Part III of Book I of the Treatise, and in the chapters devoted to this subject in the First Enquiry, Hume concentrates major attention on the pattern of inference that can yield causal judgment. He goes to great lengths to establish a noncognitivist position here, just as he did in his ethics.[1] The strategy he follows in elaborating his noncognitivism is similar to the one pursued in his ethics. He shows that there is no inherent rational connection between a cause and its effect, as well as no external impression or idea that can serve as the origin of necessary connection. Instead -- just as in moral judgment -- we must turn inward and examine the workings of human psychology if we are to discover the origin of the idea of necessary connection.

Another logical factor supporting Hume's noncognitivism is that an attempt to justify causal judgment rationally would lead to an infinite regress.[2] Causal judgments are what make possible our constructing a stable world of fact from the discrete perceptions that are the only entities present to human consciousness at any one moment. By making causal judgments we infer from the presence of an immediate impression to its usual attendant, which we have not yet on this occasion actually experienced. To use a favorite example of Hume's, from an awareness of flame, we immediately infer the presence of heat. In all cases when we pronounce causal judgments, therefore, the usual attendant of our present impression is still in the future -- however immediate -- so that the utterance of a valid causal judgment presupposes the truth of the inductive principle concerning the uniformity of nature. This principle, however, is not susceptible of proof. It cannot be shown demonstratively to be so, since the opposite of every demonstrative truth cannot even be conceived. The denial of a demonstrative truth would involve a self-contradiction. Since we may conceive of the course of nature changing, the inductive principle cannot be proven demonstratively. Neither, however, can it be proven probabilistically. A basic presupposition of all probabilistic arguments is that the future will resemble the past. It is only by positing such a resemblance, for example, that we are able to infer from the fact of the sun's having risen every day in the past to its probable rising tomorrow. Since the inductive principle forms a fundamental assumption of all arguments from experience, it cannot itself be inferred from experience.

Of the two elements of Hume's noncognitivism in causal judgment as outlined in the Treatise -- his restricting the sources of knowledge to what are generated by impressions and ideas, and the infinite regress argument which vitiates a justificatory account of causal judgment -- only the first is strictly continuous with a component of his noncognitivism in moral judgment. For the infinite regress argument, the parallel in the ethics would be Hume's strictures against deriving an evaluative conclusion from purely factual premises.

In the First Enquiry, Hume introduces one major variation on the infinite regress argument -- what one might call an argument from circularity -- which, unlike the infinite regress argument which is directed exclusively against the possibility of justifying causal judgment, is intended to show the impossibility of rationally justifying both causal and inductive judgment.[3] Hume tries to show that although we speak of cause as necessary connection, when we search for evidentiary support for this statement we realize that all we can point to are patterns of constant conjunction of discrete events. In order to extrapolate from constant conjunction of events to the idea of a necessary connection residing between them, we must assume the truth of induction, i.e., that the pattern of the relation between events which we have observed in the past will continue in the future. However, the most obvious way to justify inductive judgment would be if we could presuppose the truth of causal judgment -- that a necessary connection exists between a current impression and an associated lively idea which has always followed it, certifying to the continuance of this pattern of relationship into the future. Since causal judgment presupposes the truth of induction -- and inductive generalization presupposes the truth of necessary connection -- while neither sort of judgment can be justified independently, the attempt to prove the truth of both founders on a vicious circularity.

In the *Enquiries*, where Hume's arguments appear less diffuse and in a more simplified form than in the *Treatise*, the continuities of argument for establishing a noncognitivist position in both ethics and epistemology emerge even more strikingly than in the *Treatise*. In Section Four, Part Two, of the *Enquiry Concerning Human Understanding*, Hume adduces an argument against the attempt to justify causal judgment which is strongly reminiscent of the argument we have quoted from Appendix I of the *Second Enquiry* against the attempt to justify moral judgment.

> But we have not yet attained any tolerable satisfaction with regard to the first question first proposed (i.e. "What is the nature of that evidence which assures us of any real existence and matter of fact, beyond the present testimony of our senses, or records of

our memory?") Each solution still gives rise to a new question as difficult as the foregoing, and leads us on to farther enquiries. When it is asked, What is the nature of all our reasonings concerning matter of fact? the proper answer seems to be, that they are founded on the relation of cause and effect. When again it is asked, What is the foundation of all our reasonings and conclusions concerning that relation? it may be replied in one word, Experience. But if we still carry on our sifting humor, and ask, What is the foundation of all conclusions from experience? this implies a new question which may be of more difficult solution and explication. Philosophers, that give themselves airs of superior wisdom and sufficiency, have a hard task when they encounter persons of inquisitive dispositions, who push them from every corner to which they retreat, and who are sure at last to bring them to some dangerous dilemma. The best expedient to prevent this confusion, is to be modest in our pretensions; and even to discover the difficulty ourselves before it is objected to us. By this means, we may make a kind of merit of our very ignorance.[4]

The novelty of this argument in the <u>Enquiry</u> against the possibility of rationally justifying causal judgment, as compared with Hume's arguments against such a possibility in the <u>Treatise</u>, is that in the <u>Enquiry</u> he does not merely raise the spectre of circularity or the eruption of an infinite regress that would undermine such an effort. He questions the very theoretical soundness of an attempt to justify in the language of reasons whatever position one is seeking to defend. As long as one is speaking in the idiom of reasons, the urge to go on probing for further reasons to buttress the position one has arrived at can never logically be refused. This argument can be regarded as an extension of Hume's noncognitivism which accords reason a subsidiary role in determining one's ultimate ends. Not only in making up one's mind concerning the ends of action is the choice theoretically limitless, but even in deciding upon which principle to accept in organizing one's experience -- whether causality or some other principle of association -- as long as one remained on the plane of reasons one could not argue conclusively for any particular option. No matter how plausible the rational position one arrived at, a persistent questioner could still go on asking, "Why?" Only if one moved the argument to the level of universally correlated causes could one arrest an endless search for reasons. Only by showing that we all do form judgments in certain ways, on the basis of habits that we share in common, can we call the epistemological quest to a halt.[5]

The argument that I have just outlined in full, however, is presented only in truncated form in the paragraph cited. In the First Enquiry, Hume merely shows how any argument founded entirely on the language of reasons must ultimately prove unsatisfying. In his chapters on causality, Hume does not explicitly argue for the view that a causal explanation can remedy the defects of a justificatory argument articulated in terms of reasons. For a forthright statement of such a view, we must turn to Appendix 1 if the Second Enquiry. We have here an example of how Hume's argument in the epistemology requires to be supplemented from the ethics in order to be rendered more fully intelligible.

At this point one might raise the objection that a causal account of moral and causal judgments is vulnerable to the same attack that Hume launched against justificatory accounts of those judgments, i.e., that logically the continual raising of the question "why" cannot be foreclosed. Why can it not be argued that since it is not possible to fashion an indisputable criterion of ultimacy in causal explanations, as well as in a justificatory mode of argument, causal explanation too must be adjudged incomplete or inadequate? I think that this objection overlooks the crucial feature of causal explanations from Hume's point of view. The question that could legitimately be raised after a causal explanation of a particular type of judgment had been offered is different from the sort of question that could continually be invoked when a justification in terms of reasons is being presented. The first sort of question -- for which a "reasons" account proved unsatisfactory -- was "Why is such and such the case? (e.g. why do we make the moral and causal judgments that we do?)" To this question an account which shows how the making of these judgments is rooted in universal psychological capacities and propensities provides the only satisfactory solution. Once a causal explanation of this sort has been given, however, the question that a relentless questioner might pose becomes different -- not "Why is that so?" but "Why are we made this way?" Once it has been incontrovertibly established that we are constituted in a certain way, the only question that one could legitimately go on asking is why we are this way. To this an answer in terms of an evolutionary account of human nature might be given, but the original question, at least, that sparked the explanatory quest would have been answered.

A second argument that Hume adduces in the First Enquiry for shifting from a rational justification of causal judgment to a psychologistic explanation of it is more nearly parallel in structure to the "is-ought" argument than the arguments on causal judgment found in the Treatise. Hume says that,

> These two propositions are far from being the same, I have found that such an object has always been attended with such an effect, and I foresee, that other objects, which are, in appearance, similar, will be attended with similar effects. I shall allow, if you please, that the one proposition may justly be inferred from the other: I know in fact that it always is inferred. But if you insist that the inference is made by a chain of reasoning, I desire you to produce that reasoning. The connexion between these propositions is not intuitive. There is required a medium, which may enable the mind to draw such an inference, if indeed it be drawn by reasoning and argument. What that medium is, I must confess, passes my comprehension; and it is incumbent on those to produce it, who assert that it really exists, and is the origin of all our conclusions concerning matter of fact.[6]

There is a logical gap between the factual premise that a particular object has always been observed in the past to be conjoined with a particular effect to the predictive conclusion that objects which appear similar to the first object will always produce the same effect. This is exactly parallel to the gap Hume points to in his ethics between a factual premise which states that "Course of action A possesses naturalistic property X" to the evaluative conclusion that "A should be done." In ethics, Hume makes the double point that a bridge premise is needed between a factual premise and an evaluative conclusion, and that the middle premise cannot simply be another reason supporting the course of action in question, because an attempt at justification in terms of reasons must lead to an infinite regress. In causal judgment, as well, Hume appears intent on making a double point: First that a bridge premise is needed between the factual statement of observed conjunctions in the past and the predictive conclusion that this conjunction will hold in the future; and, second, bearing in mind the context in which this paragraph appears -- specifically, the paragraph on page 24 quoted earlier -- Hume also wants to add the caveat that a non-universal middle premise will not do. Only one couched in a causal, psychologistic idiom will be adequate to performing the task of linking the factual premise to the predictive conclusion.

A third argument that Hume employs against the possibility of providing a rational justification of causal judgment condenses and summarizes an argument found in the Treatise.[7] If the idea of necessary connection is derived from experience, then one observation should suffice in all cases to establish the presence of the causal relation. The fact that we wish to point to the number of instancces of constant conjunction of the same objects in support of a particular causal judgment is already a confession of the failure of experience alone to justify our inference. For there is nothing in the multiplicity of instances that was not already present in the first instance, save the sheer factor of number, of repetition, which awakens an internal impression in the mind. To justify the making of causal judgments simply on the basis of perceived conjunctions of events is already to presuppose as an additional premise the principle of the uniformity of nature, on the basis of which one utters a causal judgment that hypothesizes a necessary union between two discrete events in nature.

Our account of the arguments establishing

Hume's noncognitivist position in causal judgment is now complete. An almost exact parallel emerges in epistemology to Hume's statement of his noncognitivist position in ethics. If you examine the act of willful murder, Hume had said, there is nothing in the act itself which spells evil.[8] Similarly, if you examine two events that have always been conjoined together from all sides -- for example, the impact created by one billiard ball hitting another -- there is nothing inherent in either object, or in the relation between them, that can serve as the origin of the idea of necessary connection.[9]

Hume's noncognitivism, therefore, provides an identical constraint on his theories of both moral and causal judgment. It requires him to show how these judgments can be framed on the basis of irrational factors, such as feelings or habits. Hume meets this constraint in causal judgment by elaborating his notion of belief as felt determination. Belief, in causal and inductive judgment, is the counterpart to feelings of pain and pleasure in moral judgment. They each represent the affective base of judgment which can be causally explained. In moral judgment, Hume seeks to establish a universal correlation between the utterance of certain judgments and the experiencing of feelings of pain and pleasure, and in causal judgment he tries to show how belief is generated by the presence of an object to the memory or senses which has been customarily conjoined to some other object that is now recalled and posited as existing in a special relationship with the present object. The feeling of necessity that we experience in moving from the present sense-datum to its usual accompaniment is projected outwards onto external nature and serves as the origin of our idea of necessary connection. Hume could therefore say of the feeling of belief that experiencing it and projecting it outwards just are the causal judgment, in the same sense that he says that the feelings of pain or pleasure just are the moral judgment.[10]

The process of judging, however -- as we shall see more fully later in this chapter[11] -- in causal as well as in moral judgment is not as automatic as the preceding description would lead one to expect. Our capacity for sympathy makes it possible for us to frame from the perspective of an objective observer general rules which allow us to rationalize the process of judging. The emotion which serves as the affective base of judging is therefore a controlled, disciplined emotion, pruned of its excesses by being brought into line with the feelings of an objective observer. Hume's descriptions of the feelings of pleasure and pain which support moral judgment, and the feeling of belief which supports causal judgment, function as a kind of accessible norm, guiding the well-constituted individual in arriving at the proper judgment.

2. The Primacy of the Causal Relation

Before exhibiting concretely how Hume's account of causal judgment can be subsumed under a deductive-nomological schema of explanation, it would be appropriate, I think, to consider a prior question. Why should cause and effect be accorded primacy as the main associative link between our perceptions, and, consequently, as the organizing principle upon which we posit the structure of an external world? As a principle of association, cause and effect is neither inferior nor superior to contiguity and resemblance. On what basis can these latter principles be discarded when it comes to fitting our impressions and ideas into some kind of rational order? Hume himself considers this question,[12] and it is highly instructive to see how he goes about answering it.[13]

In stating the proposed objection to the centrality accorded cause and effect within his system, Hume says that according to the laws of associationistic psychology contiguity and resemblance have the same effect on the mind as cause and effect. When an object has always been contiguous with another object in the past, or strongly resembles another object, the mind is immediately carried forward from the present impression to its usual attendant idea. Yet contiguity and resemblance do not generate belief to anywhere near the same extent that causation does. We project the fabric of the external world according to our notions of which effects follow which causes, relegating contiguity and resemblance to subordinate roles in helping us organize experience.

Hume begins his answer to this objection by analyzing how we come to construct our image of the world. The mind relates in systematic fashion all its present impressions and ideas, together with what it remembers to have been the case in the past. The mind is able to distinguish between authentic memories and mere figments of the imagination by the greater force and vivacity with which the former impress themselves on the mind. But the system of realities which the mind fashions for itself is not yet complete. For it enlarges its conception of the real to include whatever ideas are customarily associated with the impressions of the senses and the ideas of the memory. The associative link that Hume refers to here is the causal connection, but before providing a justification of the mind's resorting to this mechanism of association in organizing experience in preference to its theoretically equal alternatives -- contiguity and resemblance -- Hume introduces a paragraph on the theory of historical knowledge.

He speaks of his idea of Rome -- a city that

he has never seen -- but which, based on the reports of travelers and historians, extends to include all major facets of its geography and history. "All this," Hume says, "and everything else which I believe are nothing but ideas; though by their force and settled order arising from custom and the relation of cause and effect they distinguish themselves from the other ideas which are merely the offspring of the imagination."[14]

Finally, Hume tries to explain why it is that the mind settles upon the causal relation as its primary associative mechanism in organizing experience, and, in doing so, Hume elaborates what one might call a coherence theory of justification. The crucial difference between causality and contiguity and resemblance is that a stronger element of necessity enters into the former relation than into the latter two. "There is no manner of necessity for the mind to feign any resembling and contiguous objects."[15] There is complete randomness in the objects linked in a contiguous or resembling relation. That a book happens to be lying on my desk in a room in New York does not mean that that contiguous relation has to exist anywhere else.[16] In cause and effect, on the other hand, the range of objects that can be combined with a present impression is universally fixed by which objects have been joined with the present impression in the past. Heat, for example, always accompanies fire, no matter where it is lit, or what time of day. A minimum of choice and caprice is involved in the movement of the imagination in cause and effect, which makes it superior to contiguity and resemblance as an organizing principle in constructing the fabric of an external world.

Let us retrace the steps of Hume's argument here, and see to which conclusions they lead. Hume is disbarred by his empiricist epistemological principles, which limit the sources of genuine knowledge to impressions and ideas, from justifying any of our beliefs by showing their correspondence to "something out there" in the universe. What Hume calls "perceptions" are the only entities present to the mind at any one moment. As principles of association, therefore, he cannot press for the superiority of cause and effect over contiguity and resemblance by saying that the former yields a truer picture of the world as it really is. According to Hume's epistemology, the only objective world we are capable of knowing is the one we posit on the basis of the perceptions present to our minds. To argue for the primacy of cause and effect over the other two relations by invoking some standard of objectivity which it meets better than contiguity and resemblance would be manifestly to argue in a circle, since our whole notion of an objective world represents merely our projection outward of the internal necessity we feel in moving from an immediate impression to the idea which usually accompanies it. The superiority of cause and effect over contiguity and resemblance, therefore, can only be defended on the basis of some principle of coherence. The defining characteristics of coherence, according to Hume, are conformity to some principle of necessity and an augmenting of our predictive powers. Whatever scheme of association allows us to excise caprice and arbitrary choice -- and to extend our predictive powers -- is the most coherent. The meeting of these requirements of non-arbitrariness and predictive power over our experience afford the only justifications possible for the choice of cause and effect as the relation on the basis of which we posit the structure of the external world.[17]

Having attempted to clarify the central position occupied by causality in Hume's epistemology, we are now in a position to return to the main thread of Hume's argument concerning causal judgment. A causal judgment -- that event A is the cause of event B -- cannot be rationally justified. However, Hume believes that the psychological processes of habit formation and projection can be shown to account for the making of those judgments which people previously sought to justify rationally. Hume's explanation of why people make causal judgments can be translated into the following deductive-nomological schema:

Event to be Explained: X's judgment that event A is the cause of event B.

Initial Conditions: Whenever X has observed event A, it has always been immediately followed by event B.

Covering Law: Whenever one has continually observed an event to be succeeded by another, the habits of expectation thereby built up that the second event will always follow the first, lead him to project outward his feeling of necessity and to pronounce the first event the cause of the second.

A number of modern interpreters of Hume have attacked him unfairly because they have failed to recognize the full import of Hume's psychologistic account of causal judgment. Flew, for example, criticizes Hume for failing to do justice to the element of the subjunctive, or contrary-to-fact conditional, involved in the framing of causal judgments,[18] and also for "his insistence that a reference to the actual occurrence of precisely parallel cases is involved in the meaning of all causal propositions."[19] With regard to the first criticism, Flew says that Hume fails to justify the step over the logical gap between statements of mere constant conjunction and statements entailing subjunctive conditionals. Authentic causal judgments must contain a reference to the latter -- If A did not occur, B would not have occurred; if I did not light the fire, no heat would have been emitted -- while Hume's account -- except for the first definition of cause in the Enquiry, which will be dealt with later in this chapter[20] -- makes reference only to the former.

Flew's first criticism is ambiguous. It is not clear whether he means to condemn Hume's account on metaphysical or epistemological grounds. Either way I think Flew's criticism is misguided. If Flew means to attack Hume on metaphysical grounds -- that "constant conjunction" is too reductionist as a theory of causal judgment -- then it would appear that Flew has failed to appreciate the full import of Hume's noncognitivism. Since the latter precludes a justificatory account of causal judgment, Hume can only explain in psychological terms how we come to hold the belief summarized by the contrary to fact conditional e.g., if the fire had not been lit, no heat would have been emitted. The belief itself, in Hume's view, is unfounded.

If, however, Flew is making an epistemological point -- that the subjunctive conditional must be invoked as an identifying criterion in helping us to distinguish authentic causal connections from mere conjunctions, then Hume is able to meet Flew on his own ground. Hume, too, is aware of the need for general rules to help account for the selection process that must take place in determining which features of a particular situation are to be correlated with each other. The contrary to fact conditional informs us of one way of doing this -- i.e., by suggesting a kind of negative correlation, when B's do not occur, A's do not occur either. In order to know that one event is the cause of another -- and that some third event is not responsible for both events occurring -- we must have recourse to some such method indicated by the contrary to fact conditional. Hume in Section Fifteen of Part

Three of Book One of the Treatise, entitled, "Rules by which to Judge the Causes and Effects," seems to have recognized the need for the employment of a selection process by which to delimit authentic causal judgments from mere conjunctions. An appropriate niche thus exists within Hume's philosophy where Flew's strictures concerning the subjunctive conditional could be incorporated.

Concerning Flew's second criticism, that too would have been to the point if Hume were trying to justify causal judgment. Since, for the reasons indicated above, Hume believed this to be impossible, what he sets out to provide instead is a causal, psychologistic account of how we come to make causal judgments. In a psychological account designed to explain how we come to entertain a belief in causality, the number of instances of constant conjunction which we have observed between two objects figures as an initial condition, which makes possible the invocation of a psychological law to explain our utterance of a particular causal judgment.

3. Hume's Two Definitions of Cause[21]

After outlining his arguments in favor of a noncognitivist position in epistemology, and advancing his own psychologistic account of causal judgment, Hume -- in a paragraph that needs to be quoted at length -- presents two definitions of cause.

> There may two definitions be given of this relation, which are only different, by their presenting a different view of the same object, and making us consider it either as a philosophical or as a natural relation; either as a comparison of two ideas, or as an association betwixt them. We may define a cause to be "An object precedent and contiguous

to another, and where all the objects resembling the former are placed in like relations of precedency and contiguity to those objects that resemble the latter." If this definition be esteemed defective because drawn from objects foreign to the cause, we may substitute this other definition in its place, viz., "A cause is an object precedent and contiguous to another, and so united with it that the idea of the one determines the mind to form the idea of the other, and the impression of the one to form a more lively idea of the other." Should this definition also be rejected for the same reason, I know no other remedy, than that the persons who express this delicacy, should substitute a juster definition in its place.[22]

Perhaps the most striking aspect to notice about Hume's two definitions of cause is that they really are two definitions. Their meanings and extensions differ. The second definition refers to certain mental phenomena linking together the cause and effect, while the first is couched in purely objective terms. Definition Two invokes a human agent engaged in making a causal judgment, and the laws of associationistic psychology governing his thinking, while One does not refer to the thought processes of any human being. The extensions of the two definitions also differ. Definition One covers a vast multitude of pairs of occurrences that have never been observed, which would be excluded by Definition Two. Conversely, there are situations in which an event has occurred, and where we expect another event to follow, which does not. In this case, the desiderata of Definition Two would be met, but not those of Definition One.[23]

The distinction between natural and

philosophical relations which Hume ostensibly draws to indicate why two definitions of cause are needed does not really help us. In Book One, Part One, Section Five, where Hume introduces the distinction between natural and philosophical relations, he defines the difference between them in a relatively obscure way. He says that natural relations refer to those relations that exemplify the laws of associationistic psychology. Philosophical relations are scientific, that is, the learned comprehend a relation to exist while the vulgar speak as if no relation existed. In Hume's words, philosophical relations refer to "that particular circumstance, in which, even upon the arbitrary union of two ideas in the fancy, we may think proper to compare them."[24] As if the language in this passage were not already unclear, Hume compounds the obscurity still further by stating that three members of his class of philosophical relations overlap with his class of natural relations. One of the three members referred to is cause and effect, the very relation concerning which Hume invokes the distinction between philosophical and natural relations in the paragraph cited.

We are left, then, with two major questions concerning Hume's two definitions of cause: 1. What led Hume to introduce his second definition? 2. What is its relationship to the first? I believe that the most satisfactory answer as to why two definitions are needed is to say that they are offered in response to two different questions.[25] The first definition answers the question, "What is being asserted in causal judgment?" and is couched in purely objective, non-psychological terms. The second definition answers the question, "What states of affairs must obtain for the asserter properly to believe that A causes B?" There are two reasons why I believe Hume finds his first definition of cause unsatisfactory. The first is expressed in his whole previously stated noncognitivist argument. On the basis of the observed precedency and contiguity of two objects before us, we pronounce one to be the cause of the other, i.e., we assert that in all objects resembling the two currently before us a causal relation will subsist between them. However, as Hume had been a pains earlier to show, this conclusion is unwarranted on the basis of the evidence before us, because it involves invocation of the inductive principle, that the future will resemble the past, which itself cannot be justified either on the basis of certain arguments, or even probabilistically. A second reason why Hume finds his first definition unsatisfactory is that according to his epistemological principles he must find either an impression or idea as the source of our idea of necessary connection. Since he has already shown that he cannot supply either an external impression or idea as the origin of that idea, he must endeavor to locate an internal impression from which we derive "necessary connection." "Unpacking" the objective content of a causal statement, therefore, leaves us logically exposed, bereft of any rational argument or external impression or idea to support our contention that Event A is the cause of Event B. Definition Two fills the gap by referring to the psychological conditioning process that can explain our utterance of causal judgments.

However, a question immediately arises. In what sense can Definition Two be regarded as a definition at all, since all it appears to be concerned with are the psychological conditions which make possible the drawing of causal inferences. Unless we were to say that Hume were guilty of confusing the meaning of a term with the circumstances under which one comes to utter it, Definition Two would not seem to qualify as a definition at all.

In order to absolve Hume of this confusion, we must extrapolate from his argument presented in abbreviated form in the First Enquiry -- and elaborated more fully in Appendix I to the Second Enquiry -- to the effect that any justificatory mode of argument is bound to lead to an infinite regress. In the case of causal judgment this means that it is not just our previous attempts at justification -- which involved a futile search for an external impression or idea as the origin of our idea of necessary connection, and which in terms of reasoned argument led to the citation of the inductive principle which in turn could not be justified -- that have failed, but that any attempt to justify causal judgment in the language of reasons must in principle fail. As long as we remain on the level of reasons, Hume believes, the ever-widening request for explanation -- our continuing to ask "Why?" of every reason that might be offered -- cannot be legitimately halted. An objective definition of cause as necessary connection -- like a rational justification of it -- would appear to be doomed according to Hume's theory of explanation, since no logical restraint could be imposed on one's continuing to ask, "But why should this be so?" Unless one's definition were purely analytic -- which an informative definition of cause could not be -- one would have no way of foreclosing this question. Only by moving our argument on to the plane of established psychological correlations can we logically meet the charge of arbitrariness in arresting the inquiry at the point that we do. It appears therefore that only by taking this infinite regress argument against employing the language of reasons into account can we explain Hume's reduction of the meaning of cause as necessary connection to the circumstances under which one comes to utter causal judgment, and consequently why Hume substitutes the second definition for the first.

One might raise the objection against my interpretation of Hume's Definition Two that I am violating Hume's own strictures against deriving a normative judgment from purely factual premises.[26] Definition Two, I have said, describes what states of affairs must obtain for an agent properly to believe that A causes B. Definition Two, however, purports to be a definition of cause, which means that on the basis of the psychological considerations adduced in it Hume sanctions the utterance of causal judgment. Is he not then deriving an ought -- "You (agent) ought to pronounce a causal judgment" -- from an is -- the fact that certain psychological conditions manifesting the laws of association obtain within the consciousness of an agent? However, when we bear in mind our previous account of Hume's theory of moral judgment, we realize that his psychologistic account of causal judgment involves him in precisely the same difficulty that we encountered earlier in moral judgment. What was said in resolution of this difficulty in moral judgment is therefore directly applicable here. Hume envisaged his role as that of a moral scientist. In the cases of both moral and causal judgment, he claimed to show that a relationship exists between the utterance of a correct judgment and the presence of certain states of feeling or habits of expectation in man. If to state the precise nature of this relationship was already to violate "is-ought," then so much the worse for "is-ought." Hume, the philosopher, would simply have to accommodate the findings of Hume, the moral scientist, within the appropriate logical scheme. I have already indicated that I believe Hume intends for us to subsume his psychologistic accounts of both moral and causal judgment under a deductive-nomological schema of explanation, which would allow him to state his correlations without violating his own strictures against deriving an evaluative conclusion from purely factual permises.[27]

With regard to Hume's second definition of cause itself, Whitehead attacks it on grounds of circularity.[28] Hume defines cause, which refers to necessary connection,[29] in terms of "an object precedent and contiguous to another, and so united with it, etc." He appears to define necessary connection of objects in terms of a necessary connection in the mind between an impression and an associated lively idea. His definition of cause -- of necessary connection -- thus presupposes the very idea of necessity which it is trying to define. I believe that one can answer Whitehead by saying that the shift from one causal arena to another does not involve Hume in circularity. The felt determination of the mind to move from one event to the next is experienced, while two billiard balls colliding, abstracted from our experience of them, yields no felt necessity. The "felt necessity" stands in a different relation to us than other causal connections.

In Hume's presentation of his two definitions of cause in the Enquiry,[30] only one major difference occurs. A contrary-to-fact conditional is included as part of the first definition in the Enquiry. After defining cause as "an object, followed by another, and where all the objects similar to the first are followed by objects similar to the second," Hume adds, "Or in other words where, if the first object had not been, the second never had existed." The pattern of Hume's argument here, however, is similar to the Treatise. Just as in the Treatise, the first definition was couched in objective terms, so too here. The objective definition is merely stated more sharply to include a counter-factual conditional which is neither a paraphrase of, nor is entailed by, the first sentence of the definition. The second definition -- which represents for Hume the satisfactory one -- is stated in both cases in psychological terms.

4. The Role of General Rules in Causal Judgment

Flew criticizes Hume for analyzing causal judgment purely from an observer's standpoint, while neglecting the agent's, or experimenter's, perspective.[31] More awareness of the latter would perhaps have led Hume to become cognizant of a pragmatic justification of causal judgment, as a "lever," or as "a leading principle of scientific investigation."[32] Flew's accusation, however, when viewed in the total context of Hume's thought on causal judgment, is not entirely justified. For interspersed throughout his lengthy treatment of causal judgment from the spectator's standpoint -- of the grounds of legitimate inference in causal judgment -- Hume makes constant reference to general rules which can guide us in framing proper causal judgments. This strand of Hume's thought culminates in Section Fifteen, of Part Three of Book One, where Hume provides a list of "Rules by which to Judge of Causes and Effects."

The introduction of the concept of general rules which can aid in the framing of causal judgments is no mere haphazard inclusion on Hume's part. It is necessitated by the previous steps in his argument. For Hume's noncognitivism poses a dilemma for his theory of causal judgment similar to the one created by his noncognitivism for his theory of moral judgment. Since it is not possible to rationally justify causal judgment -- we can find no antecedent external impression or idea as the basis for our idea of necessary connection; in order to justify a particular causal judgment we must invoke the inductive principle which in its turn cannot be justified -- we are faced with the initial problem of narrowing down the range of cases to which such judgments apply. In moral judgment, too, Hume's immediate problem was the same. Since reason's role is subservient to the passions -- and one cannot derive an evaluative conclusion from purely factual premises --

on what basis can one restrict the range of cases to which moral judgments apply? In Section Fifteen of Part Three, speaking of causal judgment, Hume says that from the perspective of reason

> Any thing may produce any thing. Creation, annihilation, motion, reason, volition; all these may arise from one another, or from any other object we can imagine. Nor will this appear strange, if we compare two principles explained above, that the constant conjunction of objects determines their causation, and that properly speaking no objects are contrary to each other, but existence and non-existence. Where objects are not contrary, nothing hinders them from having that constant conjunction, on which the relation of cause and effect totally depends.[33]

Habits of association can theoretically cluster around any sequences of events in nature. In moral judgment, too, on the basis of his noncognitivism, Hume would have to admit the possibility of total arbitrariness in the framing of our judgments. In order to foreclose the anarchic implications of his noncognitivism, Hume introduces the fundamental principle of coherence, as well as the notion of general rules which serve as limiting, rational factors narrowing the range of appropriate judgment in causality and ethics. In the previous chapter, we have discussed the nature of the rules circumscribing legitimate moral judgment, and in the next chapter we shall delve into them more fully when we analyze Hume's political theory. However, what is not so apparent on a first reading of Hume on causality is the number and variety of general rules which Hume introduces to limit the applicability of causal judgment. It is to a consideration of these that we now turn.

General rules help us identify which judgments can be legitimately regarded as causal. One typical case where we know we are acting upon a correct causal inference is when we act automatically, responding almost by reflex to a situation of imminent danger or opportunity.[34] An example that Hume offers is that of a person who stops short in his journey upon meeting a river because of an almost instinctual awareness of the relationship between water and sinking, and sinking and suffocating.

A second invocation of general rules occurs when Hume explains why it is that on certain occasions one instance of a conjunction between events suffices for us to postulate a causal connection between them.[35] From our varied experience of causal relations subsisting between objects, we abstract the general principle "that like objects, placed in like circumstances, will always produce like effects."[36] Relying on this general rule, we sometimes shorten the period of actual observation of a constant conjunction existing between two objects, and pronounce such a relation to exist between them on the basis of just one observation or experiment. The particular occasions in which we will invoke this general rule will depend upon how many of the necessary conditions for the presence of the causal relation -- some of which Hume numerates in Section Fifteen of Part Three -- are operative in the case at hand.

A third instance of a general rule which Hume provides in helping us to identify correct causal judgments is that what is immediately present before the mind need not be an impression which transfers part of its liveliness to an idea of what usually accompanies it.[37] The process may be reversed. I may have an idea of an object whose antecedent impression I had previously forgotten. Part of the liveliness of the idea is transferred to the impression, in whose existence

I now believe.

A fourth general rule which Hume provides refers to the force and vivacity which sometimes attach to an idea of an idea.[38] Remembering that we have entertained a certain idea in the past, i.e., having regarded it as true, when the thought reemerges in our consciousness in the present we accord it a much greater degree of belief than if we had never accepted it as true.

A fifth general rule relates to a question discussed earlier in this chapter. Being rationally aware that contiguity and resemblance are more likely to mislead us as a guide to what is real -- since what they associate together fluctuates much more widely and randomly -- than causality, we frame a general rule against reposing too much confidence in judgments uttered on the basis of contiguity and resemblance.[39]

In the section called, "Of Unphilosophical Probability," Hume distinguishes between two species of general rules, what one might call the vulgar and the wise.[40] The vulgar frame rules of thumb for the application of causal judgment on the basis of insufficient evidence, and premature abstraction from experience. With the vulgar, the imagination predominates over what Hume calls the judgment. On the basis of a superficial resemblance between a present cause and one which they remember, they postulate that an effect similar to what occurred in the past will follow. The wise -- those whose capacity for abstraction is more fully developed -- are not that easily beguiled. They use general rules in the sense of principles rationally arrived at to defeat the effects of general rules in the sense of unreflective associations drawn in the imagination. Here is how Hume describes general rules in the laudatory sense: "By them (general rules) we learn to distinguish the accidental circumstances from the efficacious causes; and when we find that an effect can be produced without the concurrence of any particular circumstance, we conclude that that circumstance makes not a part of the efficacious cause, however frequently conjoined with it."[41]

In addition to the broad maxims that Hume offers to help us distinguish genuine instances of the causal relation from the welter of associated events that confront us in daily life, Hume presents in Section Fifteen, entitled, "Rules by which to Judge of Causes and Effects," a list of necessary conditions for the presence of the causal relation which can guide those truly capable of abstract reasoning in determining the application of causal judgment. Hume's eight rules may be summarized as follows:

1, 2. The cause and effect must be contiguous in space and time, and the cause must be prior to the effect. 3. There must be a constant union between the cause and effect. 4. The same cause always produces the same effect, and the same effect never arises but from the same cause. This means that once we have ascertained to our satisfaction -- through observation or experiment -- that a certain event is the cause of some other event, we are licensed to make the inductive inference that the first event will always produce the second. 5. Where several different objects produce the same effect, it is to a factor common to all of them to which we must ascribe the cause. 6. Conversely, the difference in the effect produced by two resembling objects must be ascribed to that factor in which they differ. 7. There are such phenomena as a compound cause and a compound effect which derive from the incompatible results achieved by an increase in the extent or intensity of the cause. The example which Hume provides is that of a certain degree of heat which produces pleasure, and of its increase beyond a certain level which evokes pain. 8. Finally, an object which exists for any length of time without producing an effect is not to be regarded as the sole cause of an effect which is later produced when a new object is added to the original one. This rule is the closest Hume comes to drawing a distinction between a necessary condition and a cause, and of regarding that factor as a cause which is the most prominent of those conditions which immediately precede the production of the effect.

Thus, we have seen that throughout the long Part Three, of Book One of the <u>Treatise</u>, Hume makes reference to general rules which help us identify informally, or through the enumeration of necessary conditions, the presence of the causal relation. The reason for the introduction of general rules into the scheme of Hume's argument appears to be the same here as it was in moral judgment. Beginning with his noncognitivist principles which undermine the possibility of rational justification of either moral or causal judgments, Hume is faced with the problem of devising a philosophical strategy that will allow him to delimit in a manner that accords with our notion of what is reasonable the scope of these judgments. Taking only the noncognitivism into account, judgments of what is good and evil, and judgments of which events correlate with which other events, could be extended indefinitely in ways which boggle the imagination. To narrow the destructive implications of his noncognitivism, Hume introduces in both ethics and causality the notion of general rules. However, nowhere in the sections on causality does Hume tell us which aspects of human nature make it possible for us to frame general rules. Read in isolation from the rest of the <u>Treatise</u>, the sections on causality contain a glaring omission. Only if we turn to the ethics and read what Hume has to say about sympathy can we fill the gap in Hume's argument on causality.

The capacity for sympathy facilitates our projecting ourselves into the positions of other people whose immediate perspectives are different from our own and who would not therefore find our judgments (moral as well as causal) intelligible if they were not framed according to some objective standard. What Hume does not spell out that clearly in his passages on sympathy in the ethics, and which emerges most emphatically only from taking the sections on causality into account, is the extent to which the workings of sympathy enable us not only to enlarge our feelings, but to reorder our perceptions in the light of abstract, rational considerations. In the properly constituted individual, the effects of sympathy include not only an extension in the range of compassion but an increase in the capacity for abstract reasoning.

Our capacity for primary sympathy -- for entering into the feelings entertained by others -- allows us to experience their perplexity when we use the terms in the moral and epistemological vocabularies too subjectively. The results achieved by our exercise of primary sympathy in both ethics and epistemology is to goad us on to evolve more stable judgments from a general perspective. In this sense, the enterprise of abstracting from our experience which we must enter upon in order to articulate the general rules of causal judgment has its origin in our capacity for primary sympathy. Analogous to the relatively disinterested perspective which we achieve through the manifestation of secondary sympathy in moral judgment is the abstracting capacity which we develop in ourselves and which enables us to frame the general rules of causal judgment. Sympathy in causal judgment eventually makes it possible for us to view the multifarious associations in nature from the perspective of

an objective observer who is able to reduce the
overwhelming complexity of his experience to man-
ageable proportions by compressing and abstracting
from his experience a series of general rules
which can be used as criteria in organizing experience. Just as in moral judgment the capacity
for taking up other peoples' points of view makes
possible the institution of a correctin mechanism
which sanctions the making of approbatory moral
judgments of only those courses of action which
would be approved by a relatively disinterested
observer, so too in causal judgment the effect
of primary sympathy is to make possible the institution of a correction mechanism which will
limit the range of causal judgments to those that
an objective observer capable of abstracting from
experience certain general rules would find acceptable.[42]

    The paramount principle which the general
rules of causal judgment try to implement -- coherence -- is also arrived at from the vantage
point of the objective observer made possible
by the operation of sympathy. In order to rescue
from chaos the fleeting impressions and ideas
that are the only entities present to the mind
at any one moment, we focus upon coherence and
the notions of necessity and predictability which
it embodies as the principle upon which to organize our perceptions, and consequently as our
image of the structure of an external world. Without the principle of coherence and the general
rules which allow us to translate it into individual causal judgments, we would move in a random
world, not able to articulate for ourselves or
others which associations occurring in the world
were significant and which were not. In fact,
we can probably go further and say that without
the capacity for sympathy the very distinction
between self and other, self and world would crum-
ble because we would lack the conceptual apparatus
for forming the causal judgments on whose basis

we posit the structure of an external world to begin with.

We can detect in this notion of necessity as non-arbitrariness a shading-off into another connotation of necessity as survival. An organizing principle of experience that sanctioned making arbitrary connections -- such as adopting contiguity and resemblance would lead to -- would impede our possibility for survival, because our expectations concerning the future would be constantly disrupted. Hume himself appears to establish the link between the notion of necessity as non-arbitrariness and the idea of necessity as survival in the following passage:

> The former (causes and effects) are the foundations of all our thoughts and actions, so that upon their removal human nature must immediately perish and go to ruin. The latter (the haphazard transitions between impressions and ideas effected in the imagination) are neither unavoidable to mankind, nor necessary, or so much as useful in the conduct of life, but on the contrary are observed only to take place in weak minds, and being opposite to the other principles of custom and reasoning, may easily be subverted by a due contrast and opposition. For this reason the former are received by philosophy and the latter rejected.[43]

The foundation principle in causal and moral judgment therefore appears to be the same. Survival, in effect, proves to be the overriding imperative governing our organization of experience in both areas. Cause and effect becomes our primary principle of association in organizing our perceptions because otherwise our survival would be jeopardized. We adhere to the laws of property which Hume sanctifies as laws of nature in his political theory[44] -- and have them serve as the basis upon which we pronounce individual moral judgments -- because without enforcing them we would face the imminent danger of society returning to a state of chaos. Our capacity for primary sympathy which generates anxiety for us concerning our own future states[45] leads us to become preoccupied with issues of security and survival. In moral judgment we focus upon the laws of property and justice as a means of alleviating that anxiety, and in causal judgment we adopt causality as our primary associative principle in experience in order to further our chances for survival. The general rules in causal judgment thus appear to embody the identical principle of necessity construed as survival as the general rules in moral judgment.

If the preceding account of causal judgment seems circular, it is a manifestation of what Goodman has called "virtuous circularity."[46] The reason why general rules can only be justified in terms of the principle of coherence, and individual causal judgments which derive their proximate justification from these rules also receive their ultimate justification only from the principle of coherence itself, is that considering that our epistemological building blocks consist only of perceptions we have nowhere else to turn but to a principle of coherence in justifying whatever patterns we impose on our perceptions. The choice of the principle of coherence can also be justified in terms of the greater opportunity it offers for achieving stable communication with others and enhancing our prospect for survival which cause and effect facilitates more completely than contiguity or resemblance, since it eliminates arbitrariness and randomness to a greater extent than they do. The preceding account enables Hume to offer what Goodman has also called a "limited justification" of causal judgment.

Those individual judgments that accord with general rules must be pronounced correct, while the rest are regarded as invalid.[47]

Our description of the workings of sympathy, however, should not be construed to mean that the correction process effected by the application of general rules operates automatically. To derive this implication from Hume's passages on sympathy would falsify one aspect of his teaching, as the following paragraph makes clear.

> These principles (of resemblance, contiguity and causation) I allow to be neither the infallible nor the sole causes of an union among ideas. They are not the infallible causes for one may fix his attention during some time on any one object without looking farther. They are not the sole causes. For the thought has evidently an irregular motion in running along its objects, and may leap from the heavens to the earth, from one end of the creation to the other, without any certain method of order. But though I allow this weakness in these three relations, and this irregularity in the imagination yet I assert that the only general principles which associate ideas are resemblance, contiguity and causation.[48]

Since there is no automatic factor inhibiting the associations drawn by the imagination, the formulation and adoption of general rules can be legitimately regarded only as a possibility available to man, resulting from his more general capacity for sympathy. General rules function as a kind of accessible norm, which an average human personality endowed with a capacity for sympathy will be able to fashion for itself and follow. Their role in causal judgment is parallel to the place they occupy in Hume's schema of moral judgment. In moral judgment, too, Hume's description of the circumstances giving rise to the concept of justice would have been undermined had we construed general rules purely descriptively. If people's notion of how the scarce human and physical resources of a community should be allocated were unanimous -- if everyone automatically viewed questions of distribution from the perspective of a relatively disinterested observer, and came strictly in all cases to the same conclusions that such an observer would -- there would be no scope for the generation and application of the concept of justice. In moral judgment, as well, general rules function as an accessible norm, whose formulation is made possible, but is in no sense guaranteed, by the presence in human beings of the capacity for sympathy.

We are now faced with the problem of interpretation here that proved central in our analysis of Hume's ethics. How can one reconcile within the body of one ethical theory or theory of causal judgment noncognitivism and a resorting to general rules? The presence of one would seem to preclude the possibility of the other. How are Hume's theories able to contain both without contradiction? We must invoke in our answer in the case of causal judgment the general schema we applied in the interpretation of Hume's ethics. The noncognitivism is advanced from the perspective of a philosophical spectator. In outlining a scheme of valid causal argument, he must take into account the fact that we can point to no antecedent external impression or idea as the basis for the idea of necessary connection, and that to justify a particular causal judgment we must invoke the inductive principle which in turn cannot be justified. The spectator therefore can only turn inward and find an internal impression as the origin of the idea of necessary connection. He must remove the argument to a psychologistic plane, and offer an explanation, rather than a justification, of causal judgment. The agent, however, need not be aware of the internal psychological processes motivating him. His reasoning is more out in the open, so to speak, involving more formal, rational considerations. The articulation of and adherence to general rules are therefore appropriate from his perspective, which is that of a person seeking to organize and act upon experience.

A straightforwardly empiricist interpretation of Hume's thought -- that there must exist a one-to-one relationship between a particular statement or judgment and specific impressions or ideas -- seems to me to be misguided according to the approach outlined here. It would be more accurate to say that in Hume's view it is only by taking into account the individual past in causal judgment -- our experience of constant conjunction of events judiciously distilled by our formulation of general rules -- and the collective past in moral judgment -- our remembrance or our reconstruction aided by general rules of what social life must be like without the restraints imposed by the rules of justice and political obligation -- that we are enabled to frame the appropriate causal and moral judgments. Hume's philosophical practice consists, therefore, in broadening the epistemological base, not in narrowing it, as his frequent invocations of traditional empiricist criteria of meaning and knowledge would lead one to believe. These narrow criteria are generally appealed to in the destructive movement of his philosophy -- when he elaborates his noncognitivism. In the constructive movement, however, when he presents his own theory of how an individual agent arrives at a particular judgment, he indicates how a whole complex of past impressions and ideas, whose lessons have been rationally sifted and translated into the language of general rules, is necessary in order to arrive at the appropriate judgment in the present.

Footnotes

[1] *Treatise*, Book I, Part III; *Enquiries*, Sections 2-6, and *passim*.

[2] *Treatise*, pp. 89-90.

[3] *Enquiries*, pp. 35-36.

[4] Ibid., p. 32.

[5] The principle of coherence that impels an agent to decide in favor of cause and effect as the most significant relation linking the distinct perceptions of experience correlates -- we shall later see (pp. 106-107) -- with the presence in human beings of a capacity for sympathy -- and can therefore be subsumed by a spectator under a general law.

[6] *Enquiries*, p. 34.

[7] Ibid., pp. 78-79; *Treatise*, pp. 162-166.

[8] *Treatise*, pp. 468-469.

[9] Ibid., Book I, Part III, Section 2.

[10] *Enquiries*, pp. 46-47.

[11] Pp. 99-112.

[12] *Treatise*, pp. 107-110.

[13] As we shall observe later -- pp. 106-107 -- the primacy which Hume accords cause and effect has its ultimate roots in man's psychological capacities, mainly sympathy.

[14] Ibid., p. 108.

[15] Ibid., p. 109.

[16] Selecting resemblance as our primary associative principle linking together the distinct perceptions of experience would be arbitrary in the sense that for practically everything in the world we can find other objects resembling them to some extent. In order to be able to delimit which resemblances are significant we would require some further associative principle.

[17] Resemblance and contiguity, however, are still significant for Hume as subordinate associative principles in experience (<u>Treatise</u>, p. 109). Without invocation of the principle of resemblance, for example, we could not assimilate the case of two billiard balls before us to all previous cases of transmission of impact between objects that we had seen, and would thus not know that the causal principle applies in the present case.

[18] Antony Flew, <u>Hume's Philosophy of Belief</u> (London: Routledge and Kegan Paul, 1961), p. 131.

[19] Ibid., p. 134.

[20] See below, pp. 98-99.

[21] In the discussion that follows, I am indebted to three articles in the Anchor collection of critical essays on Hume, edited by V.C. Chappell (Garden City: Doubleday and Co., 1966): "Hume's Two Definitions of 'Cause'," by J.A. Robinson; "Hume's Two Definitions of 'Cause'," by Thomas J. Richards; "Hume's Two Definitions of 'Cause' Reconsidered," by J.A. Robinson. Although I deal with many of the same problems that Robinson and Richards raise, my solutions to them often differ from both. A primary aim in this

section of the chapter is to show how the pattern of analysis developed with regard to moral judgment is able to accommodate some of the major difficulties that have been raised concerning Hume on causal judgment.

[22] Treatise, pp. 169-170.

[23] J.A. Robinson, "Hume's Two Definitions of Cause," in Chappell, op. cit., pp. 131-133.

[24] Treatise, p. 13.

[25] Thomas J. Richards, "Hume's Two Definitions of Cause Reconsidered," in Chappell, op. cit., p. 166.

[26] J.A. Robinson, "Hume's Two Definitions of Cause Reconsidered," in Chappell, op. cit., p. 166.

[27] What vouchsafes the correctness of the causal judgment for Hume is the invocation of the covering law. The covering law in causal judgment, as in moral judgment, contains an implicit paradigm case argument -- to the effect that only habits of association and projection formed on the basis of certain general rules (which Hume outlines) are to be regarded as correct.

[28] Alfred North Whitehead, Process and Reality, a Free Press Paperback (New York: The Free Press, 1969), p. 163.

[29] Even according to our interpretation, Hume merely elaborates the psychological conditions under which one comes to believe that a necessary connection in fact exists between two objects.

[30] Enquiries, pp. 76-77.

[31] Flew, op. cit., pp. 128-129.

[32] John Hospers, *An Introduction to Philosophical Analysis*, Second Edition (Englewood Cliffs: Prentice Hall, 1967), pp. 317-320.

[33] *Treatise*, p. 173.

[34] Ibid., pp. 103-104.

[35] Ibid., pp. 104-105.

[36] Ibid., p. 105.

[37] Ibid., p. 106.

[38] Ibid.

[39] Ibid., p. 110.

[40] Ibid., pp. 146-150.

[41] Ibid., p. 149.

[42] The analogy with moral judgment proceeds even further. Just as in moral judgment Hume would say that it is not strictly a matter of choice whether we pronounce judgments from the perspective afforded by our capacity for sympathy (See above, pp. 32-33), so too in causal judgment Hume would stress that there is something inhuman and bizarre in trying to abstract from our capacity for sympathy. The structure of Hume's philosophy, however -- which in ethics and epistemology starts out with non-cognitivist, rationally destructive moves -- imparts a deceptive air of choice to judgments which Hume would be the first to admit are quintessentially human. In rationally reconstructing Hume's movement from non-cognitivist premises to "descriptivist" conclusions in ethics and epistemology, I often continue to employ Hume's quasi-voluntarist idiom

(e.g., "The mind forsees and anticipates the change; and even from the very first instant feels the looseness of its actions, and the weak hold it has of its objects," -- Treatise, pp. 109-110); but this usage should be construed metaphorically, and not literally.

[43] Compare the following passages from the Enquiries, pp. 54-55:

> When I throw a piece of dry wood into a fire, my mind is immediately carried to conceive, that it augments, not extinguishes the flame. This transition of thought from the cause to the effect proceeds not from reason. It derives its origin altogether from custom and experience. And as it first begins from an object, present to the senses, it renders the idea or conception of flame more lively than any loose, floating reverie of the imagination. That idea arises immediately.
>
> * * *
>
> Here then is a kind of pre-established harmony between the course of nature and the succession of our ideas; and though the powers and forces by which the former is governed be wholly unknown to us; yet our thoughts and conceptions have still, we find, gone on in the same train with the other works of nature. Custom is that principle, by which this correspondence has been effected; so necessary to the subsistence of our species and the regulation of our conduct in every circumstance and occurrence of human life.

[44] Treatise, p. 484.

⁴⁵See below, pp. 124-125.

⁴⁶Nelson Goodman, *Fact, Fiction and Forecast* (New York: The Bobbs-Merrill Co., 1965), p. 64.

⁴⁷*Ibid.*, pp. 64-65.

⁴⁸*Treatise*, pp. 92-93.

CHAPTER THREE

POLITICAL THEORY

Having discerned a relatively unified pattern of argument in Hume's theories of moral and causal judgment, we turn now to his political theory to determine how illuminating the modes of analysis developed earlier are for elucidating Hume's political thought, and what further light they cast on the unity of his thought. I shall begin with an analysis of Hume's theory of justice, and continue with a discussion of his theories of revolution and political obligation. After having examined some of Hume's main arguments in his ethics, politics and epistemology, I shall attempt in Chapter Four to analyze the desiderata of the notion of unity when applied to a particular thinker's thought, and in what sense(s) Hume's work might or might not be characterized as unified.

1. Theory of Justice: Hume's Non-Utilitarianism

In many histories of Western thought[1] -- as well as those devoted more specifically to the history of Western political thought[2] -- the designation of Hume as a utilitarian in his ethical and political theory is taken for granted. The word "utility" occurs frequently in both the Treatise and the Enquiry Concerning the Principles of Morals, and this has naturally led most commentators to posit a continuity between Hume's invocation of the term and later philosophical elaboration of it. However, more is involved here simply than a repetition of a key word or phrase. The doctrine of sympathy which plays a crucial role in Nineteenth Century utilitarian thought[3] also appears to be central to Hume's ethical and political thought. Also, Hume's views on such a fundamental question as political obligation would appear to have been adopted directly by the Utilitarians. Bentham, for example, when dealing with the question of the ground of political obligation cites Hume directly in order to reaffirm his position,[4] which seems to suggest that degree of shared assumptions and insight between thinkers that goes to constitute a particular tradition.

Yet, it is my contention,[5] that the historical categorization of Hume as a utilitarian[6] is too facile, in that it overlooks important discontinuities separating Hume from utilitarian thought. With regard to the doctrines of utility and sympathy, we shall try to pinpoint the import they carried for Bentham and his followers, and compare this with the meanings these doctrines have in the context of Hume's thought. Although Hume and the Utilitarians might be construed as following a vindicationist paradigm in their political theory -- since a doctrine of sympathy is central for both -- it is crucial for an understanding of Hume to realize that his doctrine of sympathy posits views about human nature which are diametrically opposed to the Utilitarians. In what follows we shall also attempt to relate his thought to the important English philosophers in the social contract tradition -- Hobbes and Locke, exploring the possibility that Hume's deepest affinities might lie with his contractarian predecessors, rather than with his utilitarian successors.

As a preliminary question, we might consider how Hume defines the concept of utility. It seems that for him the term remains a fairly vacuous one to be identified with an unspecified tendency of an action "to the good of mankind."[7] He does not appear to connect the notion of utility with that of pleasure the way the utilitarians do. One has only to compare Bentham's forthright language in the famous first paragraph of <u>An Introduction to the Principles of Morals and</u>

Legislation with Hume's vague allusions to "the good of mankind" in order to become aware of the full extent of the difference between the two thinkers.

> Nature has placed mankind under the governance of two sovereign masters, pain and pleasure. It is for them alone to point out what one ought to do, as well as to determine what we shall do. On the one hand the standard of right and wrong, on the other the chain of causes and effects, are fastened to their throne. They govern us in all we do, in all we say, in all we think: every effort we can make to throw off our subjection, will serve but to demonstrate and confirm it. In words a man may pretend to abjure their empire: but in reality he will remain subject to it all the while. The principle of utility recognizes this subjection and assumes it for the foundation of that system, the object of which is to rear the fabric of liberty by the hands of reason and of law.[8]

Hume's invocation of the concept of utility outside the context of its association with pleasure would not necessarily disbar us from counting Hume as a utilitarian if in the structure of his theory of right -- where he supplies some content to the notion of "the good of mankind" -- it turns out that the notion of "pleasure" itself performs this balancing function. However, an examination of the arguments where Hume makes use of the concept of pleasure reveals that it does not perform in his theory of right the balancing function of assigning to particular courses of action or dispositions of character their appropriate values.[9] Although one might argue that Bentham himself employs an undifferentiated notion of utility instead of a differentiated concept of pleasure, Rawls claims -- and justly I believe -- that nevertheless a mechanism of balancing exists in Utilitarian thought through the operation of "sympathy." Rawls believes that the balancing role performed by "sympathy" is already evident in Hume's thought. However, a close examination of the way "sympathy" actually works in Hume shows that this is not true.

According to Rawls, the chief animating idea behind Benthamite Utilitarianism is that "society is rightly ordered and therefore just, when its major institutions are arranged so as to achieve the greatest net balance of satisfaction summed up over all the individuals belonging to it."[10] Utilitarianism, in Rawls' view, does not take seriously the distinction between persons. All that matters from a utilitarian standpoint is that the distribution arrived at yield maximum fulfillment across a whole society, regardless of the individual sacrifices that might be required. "The most natural way then of arriving at utilitarianism (although of course not the only way of doing so)," Rawls says, "is to adopt for society as a whole the principle of rational choice for one man."[11] Since the principles of justice which require equal respect for persons are subordinate as organizing principles of society to efficient administration, the perspective of one man, suitably motivated, will yield the correct result in questions of public policy for a whole society. The single person, however, must learn to view events from the angle of vision of an impartial, sympathetic spectator, who is able seriatim, so to speak, to place himself in the position of each member of society, projecting how adoption of the particular policy would affect him, and summing up in this fashion the net balance of satisfactions or dissatisfactions that adoption of the particular course of action would yield for society at large.

Rawls believes that the doctrine of sympathy outlined and defined by Hume supports the Benthamite utilitarian conception of the good.[12] On this particular point of exegesis, however, I believe that Rawls is mistaken. There is an implicit doctrine of sympathy in the utilitarians, and, as we have seen, there is a fully elaborated and coherent notion of sympathy in Hume. However, our analysis of its role in the context of Hume's thought has revealed, I think, its insufficiency to underpin the Benthamite utilitarian conception of the good. The insights that our capacity for sympathy affords us in Hume's theory are too strongly individualistic to buttress the later utilitarian conception of the good.[13]

In assessing Hume's putative utilitarianism the significant factors to be taken into account, I think, are the following: Pleasure is not part of Hume's definition of utility but comes in at the point where he elaborates his theory of right. The theory of right places limits on the particular goods that individuals can pursue. These limits for Hume are defined in terms of the sympathetic pleasure that people feel in contemplating which courses of action to undertake or to endorse with their approval. In other words, Hume's vindicationism is pursued into his political theory and has egoistic implications. Those actions which cannot be justified in terms of a relatively narrow understanding of self-interest are foreclosed by the operation of the mechanism of sympathy from being included in the class of approbatory moral judgments.

In addition to sparking our prudential awareness of the contribution of the rules of justice to the furtherance of our self-interest, sympathy enters into Hume's account of the origin of justice at a prior stage. As I have presented it, Hume's argument concerning the rules of justice assumes a human preoccupation with issues of security and survival. However, considering Hume's theory of knowledge, he cannot simply take such concern for granted but must explain how it arises. If the only entities present to the mind at any one moment are perceptions -- discrete impressions and ideas, how does anxiety concerning our own future arise and become connected with current perceptions so that we embark upon a program in the present to safeguard our future? I think that Hume would have to explain how anxiety about our future gets generated as follows. In the present, we form images of what it would be like for us to exercise our avidity in a totally unrestrained environment. The similarity between our present impressions and those we project of a possible future leads us to posit an identity between the "subjects" of these two states of consciousness, and to regard the possible future as our own.[14]

Up to this point, however, we have merely shown how for Hume the notion of a continuous self, persisting through time, gets built up. We have not yet explained how that degree of anxiety about our future is generated which makes us respond affirmatively to the counsels of prudence urging us to accept the rules of justice. In order to account for this we must have recourse to our capacity for sympathy in the primary sense, which allows us to identify with our situation in hypothetical future states, and fosters a determination on our part to strive to alleviate in advance whatever hardships we envisage as operating in the future.

When we turn from Hume's genetic account of justice to the substance of his theory itself, its individualist stress, and its affinities with earlier contractarian theories, emerge into sharp relief.[15] Hume strongly emphasizes in his theory of justice how putting ourselves under the yoke of the rules of justice redounds to our own individual interest: "Instead of departing from our own interest, or from that of our nearest friends, by abstaining from the possessions of others, we cannot better consult both these interests than by such a convention (establishing the rules of justice); because it is by that means we maintain society, which is so necessary to their well-being and subsistence, as well as to our own."[16] "To the imposition then and observance of these rules (of justice), both in general and in every particular instance, they are at first induced only by a regard to interest."[17] "His (i.e., man's) confined benevolence and his necessitous condition, give rise to that virtue (justice), only by making it requisite to the public interest, and to that of every individual."[18]

Considering Hume's repeatedly stated belief in the complete coincidence between the public good achieved by adherence to the rules of justice and our own individual goods, it is not surprising that when he comes to describe the nature of the convention establishing those rules he should regard individual self-interest as crucial in getting the terms of the convention accepted: "Nor is the rule concerning the stability of possessions (one of the rules of justice) the less derived from human conventions that it arises gradually and acquires force by a slow progression, and by our repeated experience of the inconveniences of transgressing it. On the contrary, this experience assures us still more, that the sense of interest has become common to all our fellows, and gives us a confidence of the future regularity of their conduct: And 'tis only on the expectation of this, that our moderation and abstinence are found."[19] It is only the assurance that others will not violate the rules -- which would make it in our self-interest to be the first to violate them -- that, according to Hume, ensures the acceptance of the terms of the convention by each individual.

In order to get the egoistic stress of Hume's argument most clearly into focus, it thus becomes crucial for us to explore the presuppositions and ramifications of the fundamental societal agreement for Hume -- what he labels convention. In his book Convention, which follows Hume's theory closely,[20] David Lewis distinguishes convention from social contract as follows: "For convention, we require that each agent prefer general conformity to conformity by all but himself, ignoring his preferences regarding states of general nonconformity. For social contract, we require that each agent prefer general conformity to a certain state of general nonconformity, ignoring his preferences regarding conformity by all but himself."[21]

Pursuant to this definition, Lewis shows that the extensions of the two concepts do not coincide. The three major alternatives discussed by contract theorists might be summarized as follows:

1. The status quo (SQ), or situation of general obedience to some government; 2. The state of nature (SN), where each man must protect his own goods from his neighbor, since no sovereign is present; and, 3. Lone disobedience (LD), where my property is protected by the sovereign but where I do not contribute my share towards the maintenance of the sovereign's authority since I sometimes take my neighbor's goods. If the fundamental agreement constituting society were a convention, then the preference rankings occurring among the members would rate the status quo above lone defiance, since each prefers to conform to the stipulations contained in the convention provided that everyone else does so as well. The three major rankings would therefore be as follows:

```
    SN              SQ              SQ
    SQ              LD              SN
    LD              SN              LD²²
```

Under a convention, it would make no difference which ranking the state of nature received. In a social contract, on the other hand, the placing of the "State of nature" would be crucial. The status quo would always have to be ranked above the state of nature, with the status of "Lone defiance" remaining inconsequential for purposes of the ranking. The three major rankings would then be the following:

```
    SQ              SQ              LD
    LD              SN              SQ
    SN              LD              SN
```

If this interpretation of Hume's notion of convention as a preference for general conformity as against lone defiance is correct, then what others have called Hume's rule-utilitarianism can be viewed from an entirely different perspective. It would, strictly speaking, be inaccurate to connect Hume's stress on a rigid enforcement of the rules of property²³ with utilitarianism. In order for Hume's theory to be considered utilitarian in the classical Benthamite sense, he would have to possess a notion of the process of summing up the net pleasure that following a particular policy yields to society at large. This, in turn, would need the underpinning of a doctrine of sympathy which explained how the supreme calculator was able to place himself in the position of all the members of society, summing up within himself their responses to a proposed course of action. We have seen both from an examination of Hume's doctrine of sympathy, and from his continual stress on the individual benefit to be derived from conforming to the rules of justice, that no such notion of summing, or of individual sacrifice for the public good, can possibly be attributed to him. Hume speaks instead of self-love being turned against itself. "The same self-love therefore which renders men so incommodious to each other, taking a new and more convenient direction, produces the rules of justice, and is the first motive of their observance."[24] Our capacity for "secondary sympathy" which normally develops out of our ability to re-create within ourselves the feelings of others reenforces the rational insight described in this passage. The two together -- rational insight and imaginative grasp of the coincidence between what our individual good requires and the social good -- help us achieve the result of furthering our own individual prospects for material enrichment and survival. In the light of Hume's egoistic stress in both his substantive theory of justice and in his genetic account of how the necessity for justice is perceived by individual human beings, it seems to me plausible to connect Hume's emphasis on a rigid enforcement of the rules of justice not with some imaginary doctrine of utility, but rather with the terms of the convention itself, which require for their realization a rigid enforcement of the rules established by the convention.

Circumventing the rules of justice in a particular case -- for instance, where a poor man steals money from a miserly rich man -- and allowing considerations of humanity to prevail, would, according to Hume, not even really be to the benefit of the poor man. For he, too, is presumed to be a partner in the original convention which codified the insight "that it will be to my interest to leave another in the possession of his goods, provided he will act in the same manner with regard to me ... And this (common sense of interest) may properly enough be called a convention or agreement betwixt us, though without the interposition of a promise; since the actions of each of us have a reference to those of the other, and are performed upon the supposition that something is to be performed on the other part."[25] Others have agreed to act with the restraint imposed by the rules of property only because they relied on my awareness of how adherence to such laws contributed to my individual benefit. Conversely, my adherence to these rules was predicated upon the assumption that the other members of society would recognize how following the rules of justice furthers their individual self-interest, and would therefore lend their support to such rules. The rules would also be construed by the partners to the convention as being exceptionless in character, because otherwise the whole point of the convention might be defeated. Since each would fear that the next person would rationalize his coming under the category of the exception, it would be to his advantage to precede his neighbor in the violation of the convention. Therefore, the terms of the agreement are interpreted by each to include a rigid enforcement of the rules.

The poor man had previously agreed to obey the rules of justice because he recognized that obeying them would accrue to his individual benefit -- would protect the meager property he owned and would create the legal framework making it possible for him to improve his lot in life. His acquiescence in the rules was predicated upon others' acceptance, which in turn was based upon his acceptance. It is therefore a combination of an awareness by the poor man of how the rules of justice promote his individual interest -- together with his recognition that those rules would only be adopted if no one deviated from them -- that debars us from waiving the rules of justice in his case. The terms of the original convention itself -- which each member is presumed to have conceptualized for himself in the course of his acquiescence in such political arrangements as exist in society -- do not allow us to make any exeption in the application of the rules of justice.

I am suggesting that the fundamental agreement for Hume can best be characterized as a convention, and have indicated that Lewis appears to construe it in this way.[26] What Lewis does not indicate, however, is that Hume's account of the origin of justice and political obligation also conforms to Lewis' definition of a social contract.[27] For a social contract, Lewis has stated, "we require that each agent prefer general conformity to a certain state of general nonconformity." The convention instituting a political sovereign consists for Hume in two stages. In the first stage, the rules of justice are accepted as binding upon the members of society, without the establishment of a central authority to enforce them. This decentralized enforcement of the laws of property works well enough in a small society where sympathy in a primary sense has an opportunity to manifest itself. However, in a large society, where sympathy in this sense is prevented from functioning, people's temptation to violate the rules of justice becomes very strong.[28] It is at this stage that the second phase of the convention is agreed to -- that instituting political obligation -- in order to regularize people's adherence to the rules of justice. Thus at least the second phase of the convention for Hume represents a preference for conformity over some specific state of nonconformity.[29] The particular state that is rejected in the second phase of the convention is that which leaves enforcement of the rules of justice in the decentralized control of each individual member of society.

Since the basic agreement for Hume can be characterized as both a convention and a social contract -- the status quo being ranked above both lone defiance and the state of nature --

the only preference rankings possible for him
are the following:

    1) SQ   2) SQ
       LD   SN
       SN   LD[30]

    Hume's views, I believe, conform to the second of these two preference orderings. The decentralized execution of the rules of property that prevailed in the state of nature -- i.e., under the first phase of the convention -- was appropriate to the small size and limited population of that situation. However, when a larger society necessitates the introduction of a sovereign to enforce the laws of property -- representing what I have called the second phase of the convention -- then lone defiance has the potential of undermining the fragile foundation upon which the new status quo is based. If lone defiance is tolerated, then, according to Hume's individualist assumptions, it becomes to everyone's advantage, in order to gain a head-start on his fellows, to become the first violator of the laws of property. Lone defiance in the context of a large society has the potential not of restoring the relative degree of order that prevailed under the first phase of the convention, but of introducing anarchy. It would therefore rank last in Hume's system of rankings.

    One might say that Hume's social contract which is also a convention represents a grafting of Locke onto Hobbes. For Hobbes, the fundamental agreement setting up civil society can only be construed as a social contract, and not as a convention, because the only alternative toward instituting civil society is continuing the state of nature -- a condition of anarchy which is not viable at all. A convention, according to Lewis' definition, needs to be one of several alternative conventions, whereas a social contract need have no other alternative than the state of nature.[31] Since for Hobbes the only alternative to civil society is a self-destructive state of nature, his notion of the fundamental agreement cannot be characterized as a convention. Nevertheless, the motives prompting men to enter into a pact with each other are strongly individualistic. As Hobbes states it, in setting up a sovereign it is as if each man were to say to every other man "I authorize and give up my right of governing myself to this man, or to this assembly of men, on this condition, that thou give up thy right to him, and authorize all his actions in like manner."[32] One's acquiescence in the pact setting up civil society is thus predicated upon the dual assumption that instituting a sovereign is in everyone's individual interest, and that each recognizes that his relinquishing of right[33] will have the intended effect of promoting his security only if all members of society relinquish their right equally.

Hume follows Hobbes in stressing the egoistic self-regard that leads us to accept the terms of the agreement establishing the fundamental rules of society and government. Nevertheless, he could not have learned from Hobbes the notion of convention in a strict sense because that requires the availability of other patterns of organization besides the one the parties are instituting. Convention carries the connotation in ordinary language -- and as far as I can tell this was true even in Hume's day[34] -- that the agreement entered into remains to some extent arbitrary. I believe that this element of arbitrariness is important in Hume's understanding of convention. There would be nothing inherently irrational in Hume's view if the evolution of society remained arrested at any of the stages prior to the instituting of government. Human destructiveness would not necessarily undermine any of the stages previous to the establishment of government. It would therefore not have been irrational from some lofty philosophical perspective for human beings either to reamin on the level of isolated individuals or to live in a small society obeying the conventions establishing the rules of justice but not instituting a sovereign. In Hobbes' scheme, remaining on any level prior to the setting up of sovereign authority would constitute a fundamentally irrational choice that would culminate in an orgy of human self-destructiveness. Hume, in contradistinction to Hobbes, is careful to point out the sheerly irrational, brute historical forces that condition the human awareness of the necessity for government.[35] He indicates that it is only the fortuitous circumstance of several clans having to defend themselves against an external aggressor -- which leads them to institute a temporar˙˙ chief to lead them in battle -- that makes them cognizant of the advantages to be reaped from a central government. In contrast to Hobbes, Hume thus seeks to preserve, from a purely rational perspective, at least, the arbitrary character of the agreements existing at the root of society. It seems to me that in this stress of his political theory -- that there can be alternatives to the Hobbesian state of nature without instituting civil government -- Hume is indebted to Locke.

Locke's notion of the state of nature is notoriously ambiguous. On the one hand, Locke stresses the peaceful character of the state of nature, where we each possess the executive power of the law of nature, and can be trusted to follow and implement it.[36] Yet, on the other hand, Locke does describe the state of nature in Hobbesian terms as a state of war, since no impartial judge, whose authority is recognized by all, is present to enforce the law of nature.[37] Complicating matters still further, Locke refers to the group of people who believe that the sovereign has overstepped the bounds established by his trust --

and who take their appeal to heaven -- as a distinct unit, still capable of maintaining a degree of order among themselves without degenerating into anarchy.[38] Hume apparently opted for the more optimistic image of the state of nature present in Locke, and this interpretation influences his view of society before and after the first phase of the convention is entered into. Instead of each of us possessing the executive power of the law of nature, as in Locke, Hume pictures the members of a small society as entering into a tacit convention with each other to uphold the rules of justice. The crucial feature that distinguishes this sequence of events from Hobbes's account is that the rules of justice are accepted and regarded as binding prior to the institution of political obligation. Justice precedes political obligation in Locke and in Hume, whereas it only follows it in Hobbes.

Having taken over from Locke an image of a peacable state of nature, Hume combined it with the egoistic theory of motivation he found in Hobbes to arrive at his notion of convention. People agree to obey the rules of justice without the coercion supplied by a sovereign because they are motivated by the egoistic considerations typical of Hobbesian subjects. They realize that their avidity -- if it is not to turn into a self-defeating impulse -- needs to be practiced under certain ground rules. They also recognize that these ground rules are not likely to be accepted unless all the members of society are assured that no one will violate them, nor brook any exception to them which might open the door to clandestine violation. The social good in a minimal sense is achieved when people gain a clear conception of their individual goods, and of the only strategy that can implement it, taking into account that all the other partners to the agreement are motivated by considerations identical with their own.

The account of the motivations that lead people to acquiesce in the terms of the agreement -- and the conditions they attach to compliance -- are Hobbesian in character. The terms of the agreement itself[39] -- the stages of group life to which it makes reference -- Hume derives from Locke. My main reason for tracing Hume's theory of motivation to Hobbes rather than to Locke is that it is not at all clear from Locke's account how he would regard the lone defier of the social contract. This relates to the crucial ambiguity referred to earlier concerning Locke's notion of the state of nature. If that were indeed a peaceable state then someone who opted out of civil society could be easily condoned by the other members of society.[40] Since in a private capacity he could still be relied upon to execute the law of nature, his deviations from the norms established in society would not be that significant. Under such an interpretation of Locke's view of the state of nature, there would be no reason to include in the terms of the original contract a clause barring the possibility of lone defiance, and thus no necessity to make the terms of that agreement conform to the requirements of a convention.

In concluding my discussion of Hume's theory of justice, I should like to summarize my case for Hume's non-utilitarianism by citing from John Plamenatz's list of the essential utilitarian tenets,[41] and recapitulating Hume's stand in relation to them.

1. "Pleasure is alone good or desirable for its own sake; or else men call only those things good that are pleasant or a means to what is pleasant." -- Hume when discussing utility does not appear to connect it with the concept of pleasure, but rather with some vague notion of the public good. In the structure of his theory of right, where a definite content is worked out

for his notion of "the good of mankind," the term pleasure which Hume employs there is not sufficiently differentiated to serve as a criterion for balancing different sorts of pleasures. The mechanism of sympathy which Rawls claims performs a balancing function in utilitarian thought does not appear upon close examination to play this role in Hume, but to form part of the apparatus of an egoistic psychology which precludes identification with an expanded notion of the public good.

2. "No action is right unless it appears to the agent to be the action most likely under the circumstances to produce the greatest happiness; or else men do not call any action right unless it is one of a type that usually produces the greatest happiness possible under the circumstances." -- Relating Hume to utilitarianism as construed in this way, there are two things one might say. First, Hume defines utility in terms of a vague concept of the public good, and it is not clear if there is any link between this and the notion of happiness. Second, if the notion of the greatest happiness refers, as Bentham and his followers defined it, to the process of summing up the net pleasure over pain that undertaking a particular course of action yields to society at large, then no such concept is present in Hume. His doctrine of sympathy, unlike the utilitarian conception, could not support it.

The impartial spectator -- to whose perspective we might be said to approximate through our capacity for sympathy -- plays a fundamentally different role in utilitarian thought from what he does in Hume. Even though Bentham makes no direct reference to an impartial spectator in his moral and political theory, some interpreters have purported to see in Bentham's description of the role of the legislator a covert reference to an impartial spectator.[42] Bentham strove to undermine the authority of judge-made law, with its excessive reliance on immemorial custom and precedent, and to substitute in its place manmade legislation that would embody the most rational procedure possible for maximizing pleasure and reducing pain across a whole society. The legislator is entrusted with the job of accomplishing this task, deriving his authority in Bentham's view from purely rational foundations. Employing a felicific calculus, he tries to determine the most economical distribution of pleasures and pains across society at large. In order to be able to achieve this goal, he must strive for certainty, and remove all traces of arbitrariness from his judgments. What an impartial, comprehensive perspective therefore affords the legislator is a psychological setting within which to aim for certainty in the results of the distributive process.

In Hume the perspective of the impartial spectator made possible by the operation of sympathy does not help us achieve certainty in the results of a society-wide distributive process, but contributes toward our individual security and survival. Our capacity for sympathy enables us to recognize the coincidence between our individual goods and a minimal conception of public order, and thus to acquiesce in the rules of justice and political obligation. Nowhere does Hume describe a psychological process that would allow us to transcend our individual interests for the sake of a larger public good.

3. "Men's obligations to the government of the country in which they live, and the government's duties to them, have nothing to do with the way in which the government first acquired power or now maintains it, except to the extent to which these origins and methods affect its ability to carry out these duties." -- Hume would accept the negative side of this statement, that political obligation has nothing whatever to do

with the historical origins or particular constitutional form of a government. In fact, the Utilitarians took over the arguments supporting these views directly from Hume.[43] However, the positive aspect of political obligation -- its grounding in utility -- meant different things to the Utilitarians and to Hume. For the Benthamite Utilitarians, utility referred to the process of summing across a whole society described above. Thus, in the context of their thought, Hume's debunking of the notion of a social contract was taken seriously. Once what the state could oblige an individual citizen to do could no longer be justified in terms of a narrow definition of his self-interest, the philosophical task of justification, embodied in a social contract, had been, in effect, scrapped.[44] The utilitarians were operating with different assumptions -- with an entirely different image of the citizen's relationship to the state -- from what was prevalent in the contract theorists, including Hume. In Hume, utility functions as a rather loose and vague concept, connoting more than anything else a minimal conception of public order, whose institution and maintenance could be fully justified in terms of individual needs and interests.

Historically speaking, as John Chapman has reminded us in an article in the Nomos volume on Justice,[45] utilitarianism represents an expansion of the concept of justice beyond the notions stressed in the contractarian tradition. The classical utilitarians pointed to a strong empirical link between justice, utility and equality. Although equality of distribution did not figure in their theoretical delineation of the concept of justice, they argued that the presumption was always in favor of equal distribution promoting the principle of utility unless specific evidence could be adduced to the contrary. In Bentham's words, "the more remote from equality are the shares . . . the less is the sum of felicity produced by the sum of those shares."[46] When viewed in historical perspective, it becomes apparent that utilitarianism helped focus attention on the human needs served -- and on the level of public satisfaction achieved -- by legislation. In contrast to the utilitarians, the philosophers in the social contract tradition presupposed the separateness and independence of persons. As long as the laws imposed on men could be shown to derive from the constraints that egoists would lay down to safeguard their interests, the contract theorists were satisfied.[47] Hume's laws of property reflect the style of thinking common to these theorists. As long as the process of acquisition conforms to his rules of property, Hume regards the resulting distribution as just, no matter how vast the inequalities which are engendered. In Hume we find a new vocabulary of "utility" and "sympathy" -- which a later generation would transform into its own, more liberal uses -- filtering the content of an older tradition of thought.[48]

2. Theories of Revolution and Political Obligation

Perhaps the best way to approach Hume's theory of political obligation is to raise the question under which circumstances Hume believes that obligation legitimately ceases. The most revealing way to proceed in answering this question, I believe, is through an examination of the progressive definitions Hume offers of the emotionally-charged terms Tory and Whig, as these definitions evolve in the course of British history. One might distinguish three stages in Hume's definitions of Whig and Tory. The first attempts to describe the distinction between Roundhead and Cavalier:

> The hopes of success being nearly equal on both sides, interest had no general influence in this contest: so that

139

> Roundhead and Cavalier were merely parties of principle, neither of which disowned either monarchy or liberty; but the former party inclined most to the republican part of our government, the latter to the monarchical. In this respect, they may be considered as court and country party, inflamed into a civil war by an unhappy concurrence of circumstances, and by the turbulent spirit of the age. The commonwealth's men, and the partisans of absolute power, lay concealed in both of them, and formed but an inconsiderable part of them.[49]

Secondly, Hume describes the distinction between Whig and Tory prior to the revolution. It is at this point that the extreme positions of both parties are congealed in the "absurd principles" of "indefeasible right" and "passive obedience."[50]

With the Revolution, a more moderate tone sets into the outlook and program of both parties. "The Tories as men were enemies to oppression; and also as Englishmen they were enemies to arbitrary power." "A Tory therefore since the Revolution may be defined in a few words to be a lover of monarchy, though without abandoning liberty, and a partisan of the family of Stuart: as a Whig may be defined to be a lover of liberty, though without renouncing monarchy, and a friend to the settlement in the Protestant line."[51]

This last definition significantly fails to identify the Tory with the Jacobite cause. An Eighteenth Century Tory for Hume does not necessarily advocate either the Roman Catholic cause, or the violent restoration of the Stuarts.

While recognizing the persuasive elements

in these definitions -- Hume's attempt to limit
the partisan zeal of his own day, by painting
a moderate picture of the historical antecedents
of modern disagreements[52] -- it is important,
I think, to notice the extent to which these definitions reflect Hume's actual view of the historical past, and of the role of revolution. When
one turns from these definitions to Hume's account
of the Seventeenth Century revolutions in his
History, and the passages on revolution in the
Treatise, they merely corroborate the view of
history contained in these definitions. "But
tho' on some occasions," Hume says in the
Treatise,

> it may be justifiable, both in sound
> politics and morality to resist supreme
> power, 'tis certain that in the ordinary
> course of human affairs nothing can
> be more pernicious and criminal; and
> that besides the convulsions, which
> always attend revolutions, such a practice tends directly to the subversion
> of all government, and the causing an
> universal anarchy and confusion among
> mankind. As numerous and civilized
> societies cannot subsist without government, so government is entirely useless
> without an exact obedience. We ought
> always to weigh the advantages, which
> we reap from authority, against the
> disadvantages; and by this means we
> shall become more scrupulous of putting
> in practice the doctrine of resistance.
> The common rule requires submission;
> and 'tis only in cases of grievous
> tyranny and oppression, that the exception can take place.[53]

The image of the past that emerges from a
statement such as this -- and from Hume's description of the revolutions of the Seventeenth Century

and their aftermath -- is a holistic one, with few disruptions emerging to disturb the smooth flow of events, if it were not for the machinations of men bent at aggrandizing themselves at the expense of the public interest. Even in those cases of "grievous tyranny" where revolution is justified, Hume suggests in his <u>History</u> that the promulgation of revolutionary doctrine remains unlawful.

> Government is instituted in order to restrain the fury and injustice of the people, and being always founded on opinion not on force it is dangerous to weaken by these speculations (i.e. on the right to revolution) the reverence which the multitude owe to authority, and to instruct them beforehand that the case can ever happen when they might be freed from their duty of allegiance. Or should it be found impossible to restrain the license of human disquisitions, it must be acknowledged that the doctrine of obedience ought alone to be inculcated, and that the exceptions which are rare ought seldom or never to be mentioned in popular reasonings and discourses.[54]

With regard to his theory of revolution -- just as in his theory of justice -- Hume, I think, was heavily influenced by Hobbes. Hume's views on revolution appear to conform to those advanced by the "de facto" theorists, who were polemicists writing at the time of the Puritan Revolution, and whose literature includes, according to Quentin Skinner,[55] Hobbes's <u>Leviathan</u>. The "de facto" theorists believed that the only grounds upon which revolution could be justified emerged after the event, if the disruption the revolution introduced into society did not prove permanent or divisive. This formulation, of course, is

142

tantamount to asserting that no theory of revolution can exist in the ordinary sense of a body of doctrine defining in advance the appropriate situations when rebellion would be justified. The "de facto theory of revolution" is thus a misnomer -- a rationalization after a particular course of events has taken place to the effect that they did not after all prove too revolutionary, since continuity with the past has been reestablished. Presumably obedience to the new regime was justified as soon as its capacity to maintain order became evident.[56] From Hume's writings[57] it would seem that a longer period of time is needed -- say, the three generations that had elapsed between the Glorious Revolution and the writing of Hume's Political Essays -- before the internal mechanism of allegiance could be regarded as safely transferred to a new regime.[58]

Hume's view then would appear to be that all divisions erected in the historical continuity of a society are arbitrary -- the product of propagandists and historians who introduce them either to foment violence or as convenient stopping-points in the study of their subject. Even against Charles I, Hume believes that no prospective case for a right to revolution could have been made:

> For as I look upon all kinds of subdivision of power, from the Monarchy of France to the freest democracy of some Swiss cantons, to be equally legal if established by customs and authority; I cannot but think that the mixed monarchy of England, such as it was left by Queen Elizabeth was a lawful form of government and carried obligations to obedience and allegiance; at least it must be acknowledged that the princes and ministers who supported that form,

though somewhat arbitrarily, could not incur much blame on that account; and that there is more reason to make an apology for their antagonists than for them.[59]

Hume's vision of historical continuity forms a striking analogy to his analyses of the relationship between reason and experience and reason and sympathy discussed earlier in this essay.[60] Just as there the image of a seamless web seemed most appropriate for capturing the virtuously circular relationships linking together reason and experience and reason and sympathy, so here too in Hume's conception of history the image of a seamless web seems most revealing of the relationship Hume envisages between historical continuities and discontinuities. Generally speaking, most historical discontinuities will prove of minor importance, and will be easily reassimilable into the ongoing arrangements of society. On those rare occasions when large disruptions take place, the appropriate strategy for dealing with them is informed by the ideal of the uninterrupted flow of history. When a new system of government is introduced and manages to entrench itself, it is evident that the old battle-cries should be forgotten. An optimal integration of present with past has been achieved, and the task of statesmanship at this point is to avoid disturbing the customary obedience which has been successfully re-evoked, by not raising ominous echoes from the past.

In Hume's discussion of the basis of political obligation in the <u>Treatise</u>, and in his essay, "Of the Original Contract,"[61] the extremely narrow grounds upon which disobedience is allowed emerge into full prominence.

> The same interest therefore which causes us to submit to magistracy makes us

renounce itself in the choice of our
magistrates, and binds us down to a
certain form of government, and to particular persons, without allowing us
to aspire to the utmost perfection in
either. The case is here the same as
in that law of nature concerning the
stability of possession. 'Tis highly
advantageous and even absolutely necessary to society, that possession should
be stable; and this leads us to the
establishment of such a rule: But we
find that were we to follow the same
advantage in assigning particular possessions to particular persons, we should
disappoint our end, and perpetuate the
confusion, which that rule is intended
to prevent. We must therefore proceed
by general rules. . . .[62]

Each of us recognizes that in a large society
-- where the temptation to violate the rules of
justice is great -- it is our individual advantage
to institute a sovereign, and to give him a monopo-
ly of authority and power in society, in order
to ensure the uniform observance of the rules
of justice. If the utmost degree of adherence
we could generate for the rules of justice were
irregular and sporadic, our original motives for
the observance of those rules -- the fact that
they redound to our own individual interests;
that we assume that everyone in society views
the situation in the same way; and that all are
aware that individual obedience is predicated
upon a general uniformity -- would be thwarted.
If in a large society we could not assure universal obedience to the rules of justice, it would
become to our advantage to be the first to violate
an agreement which was generally recognized as
unworkable beyond a limited geographic area. In
order for our original insight into the necessity
of the rules of justice for the furtherance of

our individual well-being to be translated into enduring social and political arrangements, we require that a sovereign be introduced who can impartially enforce those rules under all circumstances. I think that one motive leading Hume to continually bracket political obligation with the enforcement of the rules of justice in his account of the genesis of the former is to include political obligation within the same rubric of exceptionless observance which we have previously found characterizes Hume's theory of the origin and nature of justice.[63]

> Here then is the origin of civil government and society. Men are not able radically to cure either in themselves or others that narrowness of soul which makes them prefer the present to the remote. They cannot change their natures. All they can do is to change their situation, and render the observance of justice the immediate interest of some particular persons, and its violation their more remote. These persons then are not only induced to observe those rules in their own conduct, but also to constrain others to a like regularity, and inforce the dictates of equity through the whole society. And if it be necessary they may also interest others more immediately in the execution of justice, and create a number of officers, civil and military, to assist them in their government.[64]

If Hume's theory of justice appeared to represent a fusing of elements found in both Hobbes and Locke, in his theory of political obligation Hume seems more obviously indebted to Hobbes. Fundamental to Locke's notion of political obligation is a relationship of trust prevailing between a people and the person or persons delegated to exercise authority on their behalf. The basic agreement creating civil government is between the people and the agent(s) they entrust with authority, with ultimate authority to interpret the terms of the agreement resting with the people, who as a last resort in cases of dispute can appeal to heaven -- that is, to arms and revolution. While it is true that the doctrine of majority rule serves as a simultaneous check on both governors and governed -- the former because they require the acquiescence of the majority of the "legislative" in order for their policies to be adopted, and the latter because they will normally refrain from any action including the drastic one of revolution until they have reached a majority among themselves -- the structure of Locke's theory is such that under terms less extreme than Hobbes's the relationship of political obligation can sometimes be unilaterally terminated by the governed.

In Hobbes, on the other hand, the agreement that exists at the root of government takes place only between the members of society, and involves a mutual renunciation of right whose beneficiary is the sovereign. Hobbes defines a commonwealth as "one person, of whose acts a great multitude, by mutual covenants one with another, have made themselves every one the author, to the end he may use the strength and means of them all, as he shall think expedient, for their peace and common defence."[65] While it is true that Hume's notion of sovereignty lacks the definitive attributes of the Hobbesian sovereign authority, in terms of conception of the basic understanding lying at the root of political obligation Hume conforms more to Hobbes than to Locke. What I have earlier termed Phase Two of the convention, which serves as the basis of political obligation, is an agreement to which only the members of society are a party. The sovereign is their instrument for enforcing the laws of justice, but he is not a party to the convention itself. Hume's description of who the parties to the convention are indicates, I think, the priority of his concerns with regard to the question of political obligation. Probably the main reason why Hume excludes the sovereign from being a party to the convention is to shrink as far as possible the scope of legitimate rebellion. Since presumably all the members of society are a party to the agreement setting up the sovereign, his institution reflects what they regard as in their permanent interest -- i.e., the enforcement of the rules of justice. Who the sovereign is, whether a monarch or a legislature -- and the precise limitations to be placed on his authority -- are secondary questions, the answers to which within a very wide margin do not affect the terms of the original agreement.

Keeping this perspective on Hume's theory of political obligation in view, we shall better be able to appreciate the burden of argument in his famous essay, "Of the Original Contract." The way Hume presents his argument is apt to mislead an unwary reader. He argues firstly against the historical character of a social contract, saying that most governments have their origin in "conquest or usurpation -- that is in plain terms, force."[66] Secondly, as an ahistorical theory of justification, Hume argues that the "social contract" fails because it grounds obedience in fidelity -- or the obligation to keep one's promises -- when fidelity itself has no ultimate sanction but is merely grounded in utility. Since utility also provides the most plausible justification for political obligation, would it not be logically more economical to ground obedience to the sovereign directly in utility instead of taking a detour through fidelity which itself offers only mediate justification?[67]

The weight of the argument -- how serious a criterion of justification utility actually is, and to what extent it is opposed to contractarian justifications of obligation -- depends, as I have argued earlier, on the meaning of the concept of utility. If this notion is employed in the classical utilitarian sense of the balancing of the net pleasures over pains that the adoption of a particular course of action yields to a whole society, then indeed any philosopher who grounds social practices such as promising or political obligation in this understanding of utility renounces the possibility of justifying those practices in the individualist terms sanctioned by the social contract tradition. But if "utility" is merely a shorthand way of referring to a relatively unspecified notion of "the good of mankind," then it might be possible for the pursuit of that good to be justified in individualist terms. I have already indicated that I do not believe that Hume's concept of sympathy could support the degree of self-sacrifice necessary to realize the classical utilitarian conception of the good. Hume regards sympathy as an indispensable capacity in the development of a properly egoistic individual. Such a person would recognize the coincidence between his self-interest and the minimal conception of public order encapsulated in the rules of justice and political obligation, but would be incapable of approving of that degree of self-sacrifice necessary to attain the classical utilitarian conception of the good.

If this interpretation of Hume's theory of political obligation is correct, then the language of utility which he employs is not that far removed from the vocabulary of natural rights which earlier contract theorists had invoked to determine the limits of political obligation. The scope of political obligation for Hume -- as well as for the earlier theorists -- is restricted

by the nature of the ends for which relatively
egoistic individuals would surrender their natural
rights. Speaking broadly, one might say that
for Hume and Locke, for example, we surrender
our natural liberty to do as we please to a
sovereign so that he might create a safe social
environment in which our private pursuits of
wealth, art and leisure can be carried on with
a minimum of friction with our fellows. For both
theorists, we retain a residual right to overrule
the sovereign when he infringes upon those rights
for whose protection he was instituted. With
Locke presumably the grounds for rebellion include
more than just a threat to the citizen's right
to life, but they remain fairly vague and ill-
defined under the broad rubric of a violation
of the trust binding ruler and ruled. In Hume,
the nature of the residual rights retained by
the citizen remains more ill-defined than it does
for Locke. Even the right to life loses its
sacredness in Hume's scheme. We may, for example,
commit suicide when the wretchedness of our existence impels us in that direction.[68] The limits
on obligation then for Hume are, aside from
wretchedness which allows us to commit suicide
and supersede in a sense our obligation to go
on living for the state, whatever can be construed
as a flagrant violation of utility or the public
good. Although, to my knowledge, Hume nowhere
sets out (aside from his essay on suicide) a precisely defined set of conditions when obligation
ceases, I think that the tenor of Hume's arguments
would support the following conclusion. Only
where a clear, and what one might call systematic,
violation of the public interest occurs -- when,
for instance, the sovereign does not offer the
protection of property for which he was instituted, or when oppression becomes unendurable --
when public order is purchased at a grotesquely
disproportionate price -- is revolution sanctioned. However, even on these extreme occasions
it is not permissible to theorize publicly about

revolution, but it must just erupt as a kind of historical counterpart to a natural cataclysmic event, and its results should in the shortest span of time be incorporated by the surviving institutions and structures of the old order.

In summary, one might say that the structure of Hume's arguments concerning justice and political obligation appear to be remarkably similar. Though a criterion of utility is presented as the ultimate standard governing our judgments concerning both justice and political obligation, a close reading of Hume's text reveals that the actual number of occasions when invocation of this standard is permitted are very few. Though superficially Hume's argument appears to sanction a triple-layered structure of justification --

>Utility -- public good

>Constitutive rules of justice and political obligation

>Individual judgments concerning justice and political obligation --

in reality, most particular judgments that people make will be constrained by the constitutive rules setting up the practices of justice and political obligation, with appeal to the ultimate principle of utility closed in most instances.

This shrinking of the scope of justification, however, should not mislead us into classifying Hume as a rule-utilitarian. His doctrine of sympathy, as we saw earlier, is too egoistic to support the classical utilitarian conception of the right and the good. For Hume, it is the tacit understanding presupposed by men's acceptance of the rules of justice -- that no category of exceptions be allowed -- rather than any vague concept of utility, which compels universal obedience to the rules of justice. The category of exceptions might prove too tempting to lone defiers -- who wish to reap the benefit of others' support of the rules of justice without contributing themselves -- for the parties to the first phase of the convention to recognize any exceptions at all. Since the second phase of the convention introducing a sovereign was only intended to uphold over a wider geographic area the understandings reached in the first phase, the bias against the granting of exceptions remains in force. It can be breached in the case of political obligation in circumstances so extreme that Hume never describes them in any detail. Even the English Revolution would not qualify prospectively for Hume as an example of a legitimate violation of sovereign authority. In those rare and unspecified cases where revolution can be theoretically sanctioned, it is only on condition that continuity be rapidly and amicably reestablished with the past, after the violent events have taken place.

Footnotes

[1] See, for instance, J. Bronowski and Bruce Mazlish, <u>The Western Intellectual Tradition</u> (London: Hutchinson & Co., 1960), p. 475.

[2] See, for example, George H. Sabine, <u>A History of Political Theory</u>, Third Edition (New York: Holt, Rinehart and Winston, 1961), p. 602, where, however, Hume's utilitarianism is regarded as having more in common with John Stuart Mill's than with Bentham's.

[3] John Rawls, <u>A Theory of Justice</u> (Cambridge, Mass.: The Belknap Press, Harvard, 1971), pp. 183-194.

[4] Jeremy Bentham, <u>A Fragment of Government</u>, Wilfrid Harrison, editor (Oxford: Basil Blackwell,

1967), pp. 49-56.

[5] Rawls, to some extent, supports an interpretation of Hume as a non-utilitarian. See, for instance, how he construes Hume's rejection of an original contract, in Rawls, op. cit., pp. 32-33. Yet on the crucial question of a doctrine of sympathy he posits a continuity between Hume and utilitarian thought, for which I criticize him below, pp. 123-124.

[6] John Plamenatz, in his history of utilitarian thought specifically supports this categorization. John Plamenatz, The English Utilitarians (Oxford: Basil Blackwell), pp. 22-45. See below, pp. 136-140, for a further discussion of Plamenatz's scheme of categorization.

[7] Treatise, p. 577. The specific content that John Plamenatz, for example, gives to the notion of utility, and which he claims is common to Hume as well as to "later utilitarians," seems to me incorrect with regard to Hume. See Plamenatz, op. cit., p. 2.

[8] Jeremy Bentham, An Introduction to the Principles of Morals and Legislation, Wilfrid Harrison, editor (Oxford: Basil Blackwell, 1967), p. 125. Bentham's footnote 1, which was written long after the original composition of the passage, reenforces the conclusion that Bentham was especially concerned about establishing an indissoluble link between pleasure and utility.

[9] In the Enquiries, pp. 193-194, a passage occurs which seems to suggest that Hume is thinking in terms of the balancing of satisfactions and dissatisfactions across a whole society. However, since Hume does not appear to have linked the implications of the paragraphs cited with his more general discussions concerning utility, pleasure and sympathy, I think that we may put

these passages to one side in assessing Hume's position on this question.

[10] Rawls, op. cit., p. 22. See also his article, "Justice as Fairness," in Peter Laslett and W.G. Runciman, editors, Philosophy, Politics and Society: Second Series (Oxford: Blackwell, 1964), pp. 149-151. This is the way Bentham describes the process of summing: "The community is a fictitious body, composed of the individual persons who are considered as constituting, as it were, its members. The interest of the community is what? -- The sum of the interests of the several members who compose it." Jeremy Bentham, An Introduction to the Principles of Morals and Legislation, edited by Wilfrid Harrison (Oxford: Blackwell, 1967), p. 126.

[11] Rawls, A Theory of Justice, op. cit., pp. 26-27.

[12] Ibid., pp. 185-186. "Thus an impartial spectator experiences this pleasure in contemplating the social system in proportion to the net sum of pleasure felt by those affected by it." P. 186.

[13] Supra, pp. 33-41.

[14] In phrasing it this way, I try to incorporate Hume's own account of how we come to postulate personal identity according to his epistemological principles. See Treatise, pp. 251-263.

[15] Sidgwick, in his Outlines of the History of Ethics (Boston: Beacon Press, 1964), would seem to support in its broad outlines the interpretation of Hume which follows. See pp. 204-212; 241-245.

[16] Treatise, p. 489.

[17] Ibid., p. 499.

[18] Ibid., p. 496.

[19] Ibid., p. 490.

[20] David Lewis, Convention (Cambridge, Mass.: Harvard University Press, 1969), p. 3.

[21] Ibid., p. 90.

[22] I shall argue below, p. 131, that this third ranking would most likely represent Hume's preference.

[23] Treatise, pp. 497-498.

[24] Ibid., p. 543.

[25] Ibid., p. 490.

[26] Lewis does not explicitly attribute to Hume the notion that the fundamental agreement constituting society should be characterized as a convention in his (Lewis') sense. However, since Lewis does say at the beginning of his book (p. 3) that in his analysis of convention he is following Hume -- and Hume's discussion of convention occurs in his chapters on justice and political obligation -- it seems to me probable that Lewis would acquiesce in my interpretation of Hume here.

[27] I am adopting for the purposes of this chapter Lewis' definition of a social contract, and ignoring Hume's more literal interpretation of it, because Lewis' analytic reconstruction of social contract illuminates significant continuities and discontinuities in the history of the doctrine which are obscured if we confine ourselves to the language used by the contract theorists themselves and by their "critics" --

including Hume. Though Hume vehemently attacks the idea of a social contract in his essay, "Of the Original Contract" in Charles W. Hendel, editor, *David Hume's Political Essays* (New York: The Bobbs-Merrill Co., 1953), pp. 43-61, and in the *Treatise* itself, pp. 541-545, his arguments do not affect the points at issue in the text. Hume attacks the historical authenticity of a social contract, and also argues that the promise to obey a ruler, which is supposedly enshrined in the terms of the contract, has no logical priority over the present requirement (if there is one) to obey the sovereign. Both obligations -- to obey the sovereign and to keep one's promises -- are derived from the principle of utility. Where considerations of utility sanction obedience, it should be forthcoming; otherwise, not. Crucial to the argument here, as I argue in the text, is the precise content of Hume's notion of utility, and of the doctrine of sympathy which supports it. Where a close examination of these link Hume so intimately to the contract theorists who preceded him, I believe that we are justified in questioning Hume's self-identification as a non-adherent to the idea of a social contract, and resorting to a more abstract classificatory scheme, such as Lewis', which enables us to focus upon the deeper continuities.

[28] Sympathy, even in its most developed phase, is never regarded by Hume as strong enough in its own right to overcome all temptations to act selfishly. Adequate social arrangements must channel and reenforce even a fairly sophisticated capacity for sympathy. See the *Treatise*, pp. 586-587.

[29] Even the first phase of the convention can be construed in this light. It represents a preference for conformity to a convention codifying the rules of justice to a state of affairs in which the stability of possessions is assured

by a relatively spontaneous outpouring of sympathy.

[30] Lewis, op. cit., p. 92.

[31] Ibid., p. 95.

[32] Hobbes, English Works, Molesworth edition, volume 3, p. 158. Cited in Richard Peters, Hobbes (Baltimore: Penguin Books, 1956), p. 192.

[33] According to Hobbes, in order to assure our felicity we each have a right to all that exists in the state of nature.

[34] The Shorter Oxford English Dictionary cites as deriving from Middle English a definition of convention as "An agreement or covenant between parties."

[35] Treatise, pp. 540-541.

[36] John Locke, Two Treatises of Civil Government, Peter Laslett, editor (Mentor Books, 1965), Second Treatise, sections 6-8, 13-14, 19.

[37] Ibid., section 21 and passim.

[38] Ibid., section 243 and passim.

[39] More exactly, the second phase of the convention.

[40] The state of lone defiance as Lewis defines it would not constitute a well-founded fear in Locke's view.

[41] Plamenatz, op. cit., p. 2.

[42] Jacob Viner so interprets Bentham's ethical theory in his essay, "Bentham and J.S. Mill: The Utilitarian Background," contained in his book, The Long View and the Short (Glencoe: The Free

Press, 1958), pp. 311-312.

[43] See his essay, "Of the Original Contract," in Hendel, op. cit., pp. 43-61.

[44] For a discussion of the acute problem of justification faced by Benthamite utilitarianism, and of its unsatisfactory resolution of it, see Sidgwick, op. cit., pp. 241-245.

[45] "Justice and Fairness," in Justice, op. cit., pp. 145-169. See especially pp. 149-153.

[46] Bentham, Leading Principles of a Constitutional Code, (1823), in Works, John Bowring, editor, II, p. 276. Cited in Hugo A. Bedau, "Justice and Classical Utilitarianism," in Justice, op. cit., p. 294.

[47] Kant is excluded. Supra, p. 38.

[48] For a good discussion of the change in public setting in which politics was conducted after Hume's death, see Shirley Letwin, The Pursuit of Certainty (Cambridge: Cambridge University Press, 1965), pp. 116-123.

[49] Hendel, op. cit., pp. 88-89.

[50] Ibid., p. 90.

[51] Ibid., p. 91.

[52] Much more appears to be involved in the disagreements between Whigs and Tories than Hume allows for in his definitions. In the upheavals of the Seventeenth Century, each side saw the world very differently, and acted out of a radically divergent set of assumptions. Where the Tories saw basic continuity with the past and the necessity for only minor adjustments, the Whigs perceived a break with the previous order of things

and an opportunity to reconstitute the whole social and political order of England. It is against a picture of the divisions between Whig and Tory such as this -- which occurs to us naturally and appears immediately plausible -- that Hume's "centrist" interpretation seems most quaint and most revealing.

[53] Treatise, pp. 553-554. As will become more evident below, the curious account of revolution contained in this quotation is not an isolated expression, but represents Hume's mature doctrine. The metaphor of "convulsion" in the paragraph quoted is intended seriously by Hume. The only way that revolution can be justified is when the actors creating it act out of a complete unself-consciousness, unmotivated by any body of theory to guide their perceptions, and to set out alternatives for action. Only when revolution just erupts -- under the force of unendurable oppression -- can it be justified at all in Hume's scheme.

[54] David Hume, History, IV, p. 491.

[55] Quentin Skinner, "The Context of Hobbes's Theory of Political Obligation," in Cranston and Peters, op. cit., pp. 109-142.

[56] Ibid., p. 123.

[57] Specifically from his evolutionary definitions of Whig and Tory, cited above, where it is only in Definition Three -- which refers to political divisions in Hume's own day -- that an attachment to the Catholic cause and the restoration of the Stuarts are dropped from Hume's definition of Tory.

[58] In this connection, see Sheldon S. Wolin's article, "Hume and Conservatism," in The American Political Science Review, XLVIII (1954).

[59] From a letter by Hume to Mrs. Macaulay, cited in Ernest C. Mossner, "Was Hume a Tory Historian? Facts and Reconsiderations," Journal of the History of Ideas II, 2 (1941), pp. 234-235.

[60] Supra., pp. 38-40.

[61] In Hendel, op. cit.

[62] Treatise, p. 555.

[63] Supra, pp. 127-130.

[64] Treatise, p. 537.

[65] Thomas Hobbes, Leviathan, edited by Michael Oakeshott (Oxford: Blackwell, 1946), p. 112.

[66] Hendel, op. cit., p. 49.

[67] Ibid., pp. 54-56.

[68] David Hume, "Of Suicide," in Essays: Moral, Political and Literary (Oxford: Oxford University Press, 1963), pp. 585-596. See the discussion on this essay in Michael Walzer, Obligations: Essays on Disobedience, War and Citizenship (Cambridge, Mass.: Harvard University Press, 1970), pp. 178-180.

CHAPTER FOUR

THE UNITY OF HUME'S THOUGHT

Having dealt with some of Hume's main arguments in his ethics, epistemology and political theory, we are finally in a position to confront more directly the question of the unity of his thought. We must first determine to what extent our analysis of Hume's individual arguments in all three areas yields a picture of a unified thinker. Second -- if the image of unity that emerges from our discussion of Hume's central arguments is not entirely satisfactory -- we must reconsider the problem of unity itself. Does the notion of unity connote only one level of coherence, and must every body of thought that falls below that level be dismissed as not unified, or contradictory? Are there perhaps several valid levels on which the problem of the unity of a thinker's thought might be approached? How does one determine which level is most appropriate for a specific thinker? How does one go about formulating the problem and resolving it in the case of Hume?

Let us begin with an assessment of the unity of Hume's thought that our analyses of his arguments so far have yielded. The utmost degree of unity that one can point to on this level, I think, is to indicate the pervasiveness of a vindicationist paradigm for doing philosophy in his ethics, epistemology and political theory. In his ethics, epistemology and political theory, Hume finds no form of argument satisfactory that does not include a reference to the internal makeup of an agent. It is only by showing why an agent must judge the way he does that we have provided a satisfactory philosophical explanation. In contrast to moral philosophers who follow a validationist paradigm of doing philosophy -- for whom the shifting, but not indeterminate, criteria of judgment encapsulated in the terms of the moral vocabulary set the outer limits of moral discourse -- Hume presses the argument onward from this level of reasons to that of causal generalizations, which highlight certain features in the nature of man compelling him to make the moral judgments that he does. In his epistemology, as well, Hume does not rest content in his explanatory quest until he can link up, for example, the causal judgments that we make with certain habits of association and projection that are universal in man.

In his political theory, too, Hume's contractarian views indicate a vindicationist bias. Human beings have a tendency to look at institutions such as property, justice and political obligation -- and to regularize their living together -- according to certain implicitly contractarian ways that have their foundation in the psychologistic processes of associationism and sympathy. In contrast to validationist political theorists who seek to establish the truth about specific judgments in question, Hume as a vindicationist shows why we make the particular judgments that we do -- i.e., why we cannot help making them.

Another way one might approach the question of the unity of Hume's thought is by trying to examine more closely the degree of divergence separating the two perspectives of agent and spectator that seem to influence so much of Hume's thought. It is by invoking this dual perspective that we attempted to reconcile Hume's noncognitivism with his stress on general rules in both his ethics and epistemology. In the political theory proper this dual perspective again appears to be present. On the one hand, Hume says that a rationalist justification of natural law is impossible.[1] There is no intrinsic relation between ideas intuited by the mind that can support our adherence to the rules of justice. On the other hand, though, the three rules of justice which Hume concentrates upon can be justified from an agent's action-oriented perspective, as he seeks to determine for himself the most economical basis for agreement with his fellows which will allow him to satisfy his basic drives. What larger breach, if any, does Hume's awareness of the divergent perspectives of agent and spectator betoken?; and how might one conceptualize Hume's perception of the nature of this divergence?

    The problem of the dual perspective of the agent and spectator as Nineteenth Century thinkers from Kant onwards deal with it has one of its roots in Rousseau's description of the growth of self-consciousness.[2] Man in his primitive state according to Rousseau lacks awareness of himself as a separate individual. He is incapable of doing any evil because he does not have that distance concerning himself and his activities presupposed by such standard words in the description of evil as cunning, aggression, egotism and the like. Man in the authentic state of nature is governed primarily by a drive towards self-preservation in a bare, biological sense, and by pity for the plight of others less fortunate than himself.[3] He reacts spontaneously like the other animals, with no sharp qualitative distinction separating his consciousness from theirs. Man's true and in a sense never fully recoverable loss of innocence occurs when in the course of his evolution he develops self-consciousness, or a certain distance in his activities. The moment that distance is created spells the end of natural man. Having now a certain perspective on the things that he does he is perplexed by the problem of what value to assign to them. This is where his perception of and dependence upon others comes in. Unaware of any immediate or intrinsic valuation to place upon his own behavior, man becomes dependent on others for the definition of his humanity -- for the staking out of the proper ways to act. Out of this dependence on others grows not only what men later come to recognize as true valuations, but also the endless casuistry of false ones, as vanity appears, and the desire to appear worthy in the eyes of others, and consequently to oneself, assumes monstrous proportions.

This notion of the spectator's perspective as problematic was one of Rousseau's most important legacies to Nineteenth Century thought. From Kant onwards, important thinkers of the century proceeded to develop and expand upon this insight in significant ways.[4] Kant's distinction between the noumenal self which is the subject of moral obligation and the phenomenal self which is the object of scientific generalization posits an unbridgeable distance between the self as actor and the self as the object of its own observation, which is reflected in a mutually incompatible set of presuppositions governing the separate domains of religion and morality, and science. Max Weber's distinction between an interpretive understanding of the meaning of a piece of behavior and providing a causal explanation of its antecedents and results represents a deepening of the Kantian dilemma. Under the influence of German historicism, Weber believed that an outsider could in a sense penetrate into the doings of the noumenal self. However, at this point the Kantian problem re-emerges because the historian's findings in turn are not translatable without remainder into the idiom of scientific law and generalization.

For Marx, the pristine spectator consciousness cannot have access to the truth because that consciousness is determined by circumstances of which it is not immediately aware. In order for it to surmount those circumstances and gain a true image of reality, it must learn in precisely which ways it has been warped, and a method for discounting that influence. The historicists' distinction between a practical interest in the past and an authentic historical understanding of it -- which derives ultimately from Hegel -- also refers to a way in which the spectator's consciousness can become distorted.[5] At least one part of the task of the student of history consists in learning how to divest his consciousness of presuppositions and ways of thinking that he shares with his contemporaries when he approaches the past.[6] The spectator's consciousness can become distorted through a too complete assimilation of categories of thought and understanding that belong to the present, and he must learn to discount these before he can be successful at the effort of genuine historical understanding.

Placing Hume alongside these thinkers, one is immediately struck at how foreign their fundamental conceptions are to his way of thinking. There is a nascent problem of self-consciousness in Hume, as his awareness of the dual perspective of agent and spectator indicates. However, no true breach exists for him between these two perspectives. Since the spectator's consciousness is neither limited (Kant; Weber) nor distorted (Historicism; Marx) in ways which necessitate a fundamental readjustment before he can be said truly to perceive reality, Hume's spectator requires only slightly more sophistication than an ordinary agent in order to arrive at correct judgments. Since the spectator's consciousness or perceptual apparatus poses no problems for him -- he is not affected by forces which distort it, and which he must learn to discount or to accommodate within some broad explanatory scheme -- the only mode of explanation available to him is really what is present within the agent himself if he would only introspect and learn to recognize what is governing his behavior. Viewed in this light, it is not surprising that the ostensibly non-rational elements which Hume's philosophical or scientific spectator often resorts to in his explanations of behavior turn out upon close scrutiny to be dependent upon and transparent to reason. The main example here is Hume's concept of sympathy. Reason in Hume's scheme serves in most instances as an adjunct of sympathy, in helping it expand its area of concern to include the individual's and society's betterment. Hume works primarily with a conscious theory of motivation which renders an agent's motives transparent to himself if he would only take the trouble to introspect. "Agent" and "Spectator" represent for Hume points on a continuum of man's relation to his experience whose distance can be rationally traversed by a more determined effort at introspection.

The converse of the process I have been describing appears also to be present in Hume. The absence of distorting features in man's social environment which would deflect the spectator's consciousness from truly registering what is present in reality means that in some sense human perceptions of occurrences in the world will be both accurate and adequate. Man's alienation from the world which forms so crucial a theme in the movement of thought beginning with Rousseau seems very far removed from Hume's vision of man. Instead -- just as in Adam Smith -- we find exhibited in Hume's philosophy the triumph of happy coincidence. Just as for Smith a benevolent Designer of Nature assures the total coincidence between the individual pursuit of private good and collective well-being (Smith's famous "unseen hand"), so too for Hume we must attribute to the benevolence of the Designer of Nature the fact that a rampantly intellectualistic non-cognitivism[7] is limited in such a way by the components of man's psychological makeup that he is enabled to adjust most agreeably to the requirements of living in the world.[8] Hume's "unseen hand" guarantees the congruence between human propensities and capacities and the necessities of living.

Another aspect of Hume's thought can I think be most revealingly seen from the perspective of the agent-spectator distinction which I have been describing. When we consider Hume's theory of revolution, we are struck at how impoverished his concept of action is. He seems to have no notion of heroic, transformative action.[9] It would appear that an awareness of a distance and tension between an acting and an observing self serves as a motivating factor making large-scale, innovative action possible. The need, in Sartrian language, to make the for-itself (action) and the in-itself (thought) coincide,[10] propels man onward in the creation of increasingly grandiose structures in the external world, in the hope that they might endure, and attest once and for all to the congruence of thought and action.

The unity of Hume's thought, then, can also be argued for on these negative grounds. Though a distinction between the perspectives of agent and spectator appears crucial for an understanding of his thought, the gap created between these two different ways of looking at the world seems entirely unproblematic for him. Hume's vaunted natural capacities, psychological predispositions, etc., turn out upon close examination to represent little more than reified rational capacities that do not carry his investigation of human nature beyond the conscious level. All the agent has to do is develop his powers of introspection in order to attain to the generalizations that the spectator typically makes from his own, slightly more distant perspective. On Hume's view, however, the agent-spectator distinction appears doubly fortuitous. Not only does it turn out that without much effort the agent's and spectator's perspectives can be made to coincide, but the structure of the world seems to be responsive to the particular constellation of capacities and dispositions that go to make up the ordinary man. The unity of Hume's thought might thus be held to reside in the natural transitions Hume envisages between the mental apparatus of an agent and that of a spectator, and between these and the accommodating structures of the world.[11]

With these considerations in view, perhaps the literary form of the <u>Treatise</u> itself can be seen in a new light. Hume has generally been taken at his word that he was presenting a systematic view of human nature, and the <u>Treatise</u> has usually been regarded as a contribution to systematic philosophicaal discourse. However, our investigation thus far reveals that the level of unity achieved by Hume is tenuous. Though there is a strict continuity between the vindicationist paradigm that Hume follows in his ethics, politics and epistemology, we still do not have an adequate handle on the unity of Hume's thought, because the notion of paradigm itself is perhaps too vague to give us that.[12] Also, Hume's employment of the agent-spectator distinction opens up no radical breaches in his thought; in fact, it points to a remarkable congruity between man and the world. Nevertheless, the argument for unity still remains on a fairly negative level, since we have indicated how potentially conflicting elements are reconciled in his thought, without presenting a thesis through which whatever unity resides in Hume can be most fruitfully expressed.

The most that I can find in Hume in terms of rhetorical unity[13] is a recurrent pattern of argument which is employed in the diverse areas of his thought. The pattern I think can be studied to fullest advantage in <u>The Dialogues Concerning Natural Religion</u>,[14] since the pattern's probable roots in Hume's inner conflicts emerges most clearly there. <u>The Dialogues</u> are remarkable on at least two counts. They represent the

classic attack on the Argument from Design, which
dominated popular consciousness on the question
of God's existence during the Eighteenth Century;
and they contain a central contradiction which
on the surface appears to vitiate the whole critique. Hume's criticism of the Argument from
Design is multi-faceted, but one of its main
points is the following. When we reason about
God, the subject of our discussion is a being
wholly other from man, whose attributes cannot
possibly bear the remotest analogy to the subjects
of ordinary human discourse. Therefore, the Argument from Design is defective from the start.
It can instruct us concerning possible beings
and occurrences in the recognizably human world,
but it cannot illuminate anything at all concerning a supposed being who by definition differs
from all things human.[15] In the twelfth and final
part of The Dialogues, however, Hume makes the
following statement:

> You in particular Cleanthes with whom
> I have an unreserved intimacy: You
> are sensible that notwithstanding the
> freedom of my conversation and my love
> of singular arguments, no one has a
> deeper sense of religion impressed on
> his mind, or pays a more profound adora-
> tion to the divine Being, as he discov-
> ers himself to reason, in the inexplica-
> ble contrivance and artifice of nature.
> A purpose, an intention, a design
> strikes everywhere the most careless,
> the most stupid thinker; and no man
> can be so hardened in absurd systems
> as at all times to reject it.[16]

The main spokesman in The Dialogues for Hume's
attack against the Argument from Design, Philo,
is the same speaker who makes the above statement.[17] Hume had apparently reconciled in his
own mind both the criticism and support of a

belief in God expressed by Philo. How did he achieve this? I think that a clue can be gleaned for answering this question from the last statement in the quotation: "And no man can be so hardened in absurd systems as at all times to reject it." The earlier criticism of the Argument from Design only showed that a philosophical justification for belief in God could not survive rational scrutiny. However, this did not mean that belief was not in some other sense justified. The passage quoted indicates I think in what sense Hume regards belief to be justified. Man is so constituted that he cannot "at all times" reject belief in God. In non-philosophical moments, when he responds spontaneously to the order and balance in the universe, he cannot help being overcome by awe, and attributing the origin of what impresses him to a Designer of Nature. There is an extra-philosophical level on which belief in God is entirely natural. The sentiments of wonder and awe belong just as much in the repertoire of responses of the well-constituted individual as the ability to pursue an argument through to its logical conclusion. Only a picture of man that can render each aspect of his nature its due can claim to be fully comprehensive and true to the facts.

What does this striving towards comprehensiveness reveal to us about Hume's own psychological makeup? Hume suffered a severe psychological crisis in late adolescence during which he renounced once and for all his allegiance to the Calvinism of his youth. The Treatise represents a kind of end-product, marking the resolution of that crisis.[18] The crisis itself, however, most likely revolved around the issue of religious belief, and it is in its approach to this issue, I think, that The Dialogues have a great deal to teach us about the nature of Hume's resolution of his profound early crisis. What they show, I think, is that Hume did not straightforwardly reject belief in God and move on immediately to deal with an agenda of philosophical problems in a critical, fully liberated spirit. His response was much more complex than that. He made what might be called "a separate peace" with religion, temporizing with it rather than overthrowing it entirely. He apparently felt the need to compensate for his boldness in attacking religion by an equally forthright act of reconstruction. If religious belief could no longer be rationally justified, it could at least in attenuated form be rehabilitated on a plane of natural belief.[19] Man was so constituted that he could not help believing in some sense in God. What could not be rationally supported was now reconstituted as a manifestation of a natural attribute or capacity in man.

This rationally destructive-naturalistically rehabilitative pattern of argument reappears throughout Hume's philosophy. In his epistemology, for example, though he claims that causal judgments cannot be rationally justified, we are so constituted, he believes, through our habits of association and projection that we cannot help making causal judgments. Similarly, though in his meta-ethics he argues that the only pattern of inference that is philosophically acceptable is one that derives an evaluative conclusion from at least one premise that invokes a causal law or generalization, in his ethics proper he describes an agent's evaluative judgments as deriving from his perception of certain facts mediated only through his capacity for sympathy. In his theory of justice as well, though Hume shows that a rationalistic justification of the rules of justice is impossible, nevertheless these rules have sufficient grounding in the needs and capacities of men.

Aside from two major exceptions which I will refer to shortly,[20] we thus see that a recurring

pattern of argument marks Hume's philosophy. This
pattern sheds light I believe on the most satisfactory way to view the question of the unity
of Hume's thought. Perhaps to regard the <u>Treatise</u>
as a genuinely philosophical work is misconceived
at the outset. Maybe the most illuminating way
to approach the work is as a series of essays,
held together by Hume's commitment to fusing and
expanding the intellectual legacy of certain of
his predecessors, and his attempt to apply this
legacy to a series of problems in turn with not
altogether compatible results.

    Considering Hume's occupancy of what one
might label a metaphysically middle position,
the attraction that the essay form held for him
should not be surprising.[21] The essay form has
as its backdrop the influence of the time dimension -- circumstances change, people's expectations are modified, and consequently the provisional norms which they adopt for themselves and
their societies are also altered. The essay form
is particularly appropriate for capturing the
relationship between an author theorizing about
the implications of the unstable flux of events,
and an audience searching for practical guidance
concerning how to orient itself in this situation.
Philosophy, by contrast, is written against a
background of timelessness. What matters in philosophy is the cogency of the arguments, not the
influence of historical circumstances. Hume,
however, who metaphysically occupied a kind of
middle position -- between a relentless pursuit
of philosophical argument and a rehabilitation
of ordinary belief on a naturalistic plane --
found the essay form more congenial for his purposes than a philosophical mode of discourse,
since it provides a kind of literary analogue
for his metaphysical state. In the essay form
the writer can address himself to ultimate issues,
but only in the context of the constraints imposed
by the ordinary human condition -- where time

ravages or at the very least modifies the effects of the most grandiose human constructions in both thought and politics, and where the necessity to simply go on living and making do drives one beyond the most thorny philosophical impasse.[22]

Hume, in the Treatise, appears to be dominated by three main conceptions:[23] Hutcheson's view of moral and aesthetic judgments as nonrational, resting exclusively on feeling; Newton's scientific methodology; and Locke's distinction between knowledge, and opinion and belief. Hume's ostensible plan in the Treatise was to combine and expand the teachings of all three men in order to provide a comprehensive approach to the human sciences. Hume wanted to broaden the scope of Hutcheson's teaching of the primacy of feeling over reason in the framing of moral and aesthetic judgments to include epistemological judgments as well. Part of the strategy he employed for achieving this lay in utilizing Locke's distinction between true knowledge and opinion and belief. Hume shows how most of our epistemological judgments can only be subsumed under the latter categories, and proceeds from thence to point out their roots in human feelings, habits of association, etc. Newton is important for Hume in the sense that he taught him that the first task of philosophy is by the method of analysis to determine what the fundamental experiences in nature are and then by the method of synthesis to show how in terms of these fundamental experiences others of a more derivative kind can be explained. The Newtonian aspect of Hume's teaching is evident in his desire to show how universal the scope of associationistic psychology was, how it served as the most satisfactory framework of explanation for the judgments that we make affecting all areas of human life.

In the Treatise Hume takes this conglomeration of models and aspirations and applies them concretely to one problem after another in epistemology, ethics and politics. After tackling one problem to the best of his ability, he moves on to the next, without appearing to be concerned about the implications of his individual solutions for the whole range of commitments from which he started. Some of the major contradictions in the **Treatise** pointed out in previous chapters result from Hume's failure to weld into a coherent position the disparate doctrines that influenced him. The ostensible contradiction within Hume's meta-ethics referred to earlier -- he denies the logical legitimacy of deriving an evaluative conclusion from factual premises, and yet he bases moral judgments on particular sentiments in man -- may be viewed as manifesting a tension between the Newtonian and Hutchesonian elements in his thought. The strictures against deriving an "ought" from an "is" form part of his scientific program of establishing a universal pattern of argument that can constrain judgment in all areas of human thought. Locating the missing premise in feeling manifests Hutcheson's influence. The contradiction between the meta-ethics and the ethics discussed above -- between saying on the one hand that correct moral judgments must follow a set pattern of argument which includes a universal causal premise, and deriving on the other hand key judgments in ethics and politics directly from certain facts about human nature -- betokens a tension between Newtonian and Lockean influences in Hume's thought. Newton had stressed in his scientific methodology the principle of economy, which led Hume to try and fit all human judgments into one basic mold. Locke, however, had emphasized the sufficiency of belief and opinion -- which epistemologically rank below knowledge in the true sense -- for helping man achieve his bearings in the world, and attaining success in his ordinary endeavors. The awareness of the conditions of limited benevolence and relative scarcity from which the ordinary citizen jumps to approval of the institution and enforcement of the rules of justice can be seen as counterparts in Hume to Locke's "opinion" or "belief" which are sufficient for helping us orient ourselves in the world.

When one considers Hume's systematic pretensions, one is struck by the "notebook," provisional character of the Treatise. The work as we have it appears as if it could serve only as a rough draft for the systematic, finished philosophical edifice that Hume officially intended. What we have is a philosopher's outward design for the work, but only an essayist's execution. Hume is not unique in the history of British empiricist thought in his preference for the essay form. Locke's major epistemological work is called, of course, An Essay Concerning Human Understanding, and Rosalie Colie has pointed out how integral the rhetorical possibilities of that form were to Locke's design and achievement in the Essay.[25] Hume had also composed throughout his mature life essays on moral, political and literary themes, which indicates an abiding attachment to the essay as the most suitable literary vehicle for his thought on a wide range of subjects. Many of the political essays are written from a crypto-actor's perspective, from the vantage point of a statesman having to decide on the wisest course of action in a political arena fraught with unpalatable alternatives from all sides.[26] The choice of the essay form suggests in these instances again that metaphysically Hume occupies a kind of intermediate position -- between broad political principles such as the furtherance of freedom and liberty at one extreme, and the exigencies of concrete political situations which often require the modification of those principles at the other.

There are two exceptions to the rationally destructive-naturalistically rehabilitative pattern of argument that I discern in Hume's thought, and they occur significantly in two essays. One is the essay on miracles which is incorporated as part of the <u>Enquiry Concerning Human Understanding</u>,[27] and the other is contained in his essay on suicide.[28] Hume tries to rationally undermine belief in miracles and the sanctity of human life without rehabilitating these beliefs on a naturalistic plane. Apparently the exercise of philosophical criticism is not purely reconstructive. There are some beliefs which when rationally impugned deserve to be expelled entirely from human consciousness. The essay form, unlike the systematic philosophic one, is a genre where inconsistencies such as these can pass almost without notice.

The style of thinking, philosophical concerns and presuppositions of British empiricism seem to have deep affinities with the conventions that had clustered about the essay form. For Locke, the whole conception of philosophy, and indeed of knowledge itself, must be reordered to conform to man's middling condition:

> The infinite wise Contriver of us and all things about us both fitted our senses, faculties and organs to the conveniences of life, and the business we have to do here. . . . We are furnished with faculties (dull and weak as they are) to discover enough in the creatures to lead us to the knowledge of the Creator and the knowledge of our duty, and we are fitted well enough with abilities to provide for the conveniences of living: these are our business in this world.[29]

In a sense what Locke did was to lower the sights of philosophy to conform to what he regarded as the typical and appropriate condition of man in this world. Man was ideally constituted to do certain things and achieve a particular level of knowledge, and it was the job of the philosopher to clarify his agenda under the former category, and to stake out the limits of the latter. Remaining within those limits to which the Author of Nature had assigned him, man would achieve that degree of happiness of which he was capable, since there would exist a perfect congruence between his actual capacities, a proper scientific understanding of them and the requirements of living in the world.

Hume echoes Locke in this regard, since he too emphasizes the congruence that exists between the judgments of an agent, the pattern of argument sanctioned by a philosophically or scientifically trained spectator and the requirements of living in the world. What has happened as a result of the empiricist transvaluation of values (in comparison with medieval and Renaissance Weltanschaungen)[30] is that philosophy got lost in the shuffle. The universe -- according to the sharply reduced terms in which the enterprise of understanding the world was feasible at all -- made sense to Locke and to Hume. This is why doing philosophy becomes redundant for them. Philosophy -- in one of its most hallowed and persistent senses -- represents a ceaseless searching after inter-connections in an effort to reconstitute the foundations of man and the world anew in thought. In political philosophy this architectonic impulse is also expressed in a desire to refashion the actual world by stating fresh possibilities. Viewed in this light, an empiricist philosophy is almost a contradiction in terms. Our only example of it is to be found in Hobbes, and his is an only incompletely empiricist philosophy. For an authentically skeptical thinker such as Hume, however -- who refuses to take the presuppositions of his own skepticism seriously -- philosophy becomes unavailable as a mode of discourse. "A true skeptic will be diffident of his philosophical doubts as well as of his philosophical conviction; and will never refuse any innocent satisfaction which offers itself upon account of either of them."[31]

Footnotes

[1] He also says of course, as we indicated in Chapter Two, that a rationalistic justification of the scientific laws of nature is impossible.

[2] Jean-Jacques Rousseau, *The First and Second Discourses*, edited by Roger D. Masters (New York: St. Martin's Press, 1964), *Second Discourse*, pp. 104-141.

[3] *Ibid.*, p. 130.

[4] For a discussion of the problem of consciousness in the Nineteenth Century which parallels in some respects the one in the text see Leonard Binder's essay, "Crises of Political Development," in *Crises and Sequences in Political Development* (Princeton: Princeton University Press, 1971), pp. 18-20.

[5] Michael Oakeshott, "The Activity of Being an Historian," in *Rationalism in Politics* (New York: Basic Books, 1962), pp. 137-167.

[6] Another aspect of the dialectical effort required to achieve historical understanding which the historicists stressed is opposed to this one. It consists in the conscious use of one's inheritance as clues.

[7] Unaffected, that is, by considerations of what is most conducive to human security and survival.

[8] Even though an "unseen hand" enters for

Smith and for Hume at different stages of their
argument, the fortuitous process they describe
can, I think, legitimately be referred to by the
same term. For Smith, an "unseen hand" operates
without any conscious design at all on the part
of the members of society. It just works out
that their various activities are meshed together
for their own and society's good. For Hume,
on the other hand, there is a conscious process
of calculation going on in the minds of individual
citizens concerning what would be conducive to
their own well-being. The "unseen hand" for Hume
functions on this conscious level to ensure that
what is available to human conscious perception
is all that is needed to safeguard the individual's and society's interests.

[9] Compare Leo Braudy, Narrative Form in
History and Fiction: Hume, Fielding and Gibbon
(Princeton: Princeton University Press, 1970),
pp. 31-90. Braudy says that as Hume's History
progresses, the emphasis on character as a causative factor in history diminishes, and greater
stress is laid on elements that are more conducive to the tracing and reenforcing of continuities -- laws and institutions -- as primary causative factors in history.

[10] Jean-Paul Sartre, Being and Nothingness,
Translated by Hazel Barnes (London: Methuen,
1957), Part II. For a good discussion of this
aspect of Sartre's teaching see Mary Warnock,
The Philosophy of Sartre (London: Hutchinson,
1965), Chapter Two.

[11] Some of those who have argued against the
possibility of a scientific study of politics
have sought to collapse the agent-spectator distinction -- which forms a vital pre-supposition
of such a study -- into a pre-Nineteenth Century,
Humean unity. Here, for example, is Alasdair

MacIntyre:

> The political scientist may claim to know more (quantitatively as it were) than many political agents; but his knowledge is not of a different kind, and there seems no reason to believe that the chances that he will be able to apply the inductively grounded maxims which he derives from his studies in the course of political action successfully are any higher than they are for any other political agent.

Alasdair MacIntyre, "Is a Science of Comparative Politics Possible?" in Peter Laslett, W.G. Runciman and Quentin Skinner, editors, Philosophy, Politics and Society, Fourth Series (Oxford: Blackwell, 1972), p. 23.

[12] Vindicationism represents at most what Margaret Masterman has called a metaphysical or meta-paradigm. In her article, "The Nature of a Paradigm" [in Imre Lakatos and Alan Musgrave, editors, Criticism and the Growth of Knowledge (Cambridge: Cambridge University Press, 1970), pp. 58-89] Masterman shows through close textual analysis that the twenty-one senses of "paradigm" that Thomas Kuhn employs in his book, The Structure of Scientific Revolutions [(Chicago: Chicago University Press, 1962)] fall into three main categories:

1. Metaphysical paradigm of meta-paradigm. This term encompasses those occasions in his book when Kuhn equates "paradigm" with a set of beliefs (p. 4), with a myth (p. 2), with a successful metaphysical speculation (p. 17), with a standard (p. 102), with a new way of seeing (pp. 117-121), with an organizing principle governing perception itself (p. 120), with a map (p. 108), with something that determines a large area of

reality (p. 128), and as a general epistemological viewpoint (p. 120). Masterman contrasts this use of "paradigm" which generates the most trouble in the eyes of Kuhn's critics with two other general senses in which Kuhn employs the term. 2. Sociological paradigm, as when Kuhn refers to "paradigm" as a universally recognized scientific achievement (p. X), as a concrete scientific achievement (pp. 10-11), as like a set of political institutions (p. 91), and as like also to an accepted judicial decision (p. 23). 3. Kuhn's most concrete usage of "paradigm" as an actual textbook or classic work (p. 9), as supplying tools (pp. 37 and 76), as actual instrumentation (pp. 59 and 60), etc., Masterman labels as artefact paradigms or construct paradigms (Masterman, in Lakatos and Musgrave, op. cit., p. 65). In this tri-partite division, vindicationism can only be included under the first rubric -- metaphysical paradigm or meta-paradigm -- the vaguest and least clearly defined category of the three.

[13] I am contrasting "rhetorical" here with "substantive."

[14] David Hume, Dialogues Concerning Natural Religion, edited by Norman Kemp Smith, The Library of Liberal Arts (New York: The Bobbs-Merrill Co., 1947).

[15] Ibid., p. 186.

[16] Ibid., p. 214.

[17] The above statement is not isolated, but its spirit seems to inform the whole twelfth part of the Dialogues.

[18] See the letter that Hume wrote to his physician, cited in Norman Kemp Smith, The Philosophy of David Hume (London: Macmillan, 1966), pp. 14-16; and see Letwin's chapter on "The Kirk,"

op. cit., pp. 18-28.

[19] The form of belief is attenuated because all that our sense of awe engenders for Hume is belief in some sort of prime mover of the universe, not in a personal, providential God, that punishes and rewards human beings directly for their sins and virtuous acts in this world, and who imparts a meaning and design to history. See the Dialogues, op. cit., pp. 201-202.

[20] See below, p. 176.

[21] For an historical account of the rise of the essay form in England, see Elbert N.S. Thompson, The Seventeenth Century English Essay (New York: Haskell House Publishers, 1967). Thompson summarizes the rise of the essay form as follows: "The essay, furthermore, came to reflect as the century wore on England's weariness of harsh disputes and open dissensions. For the old-time rigid dogmatism there was substituted a genial, tolerant rationalism that foretold the plain, practical ethics of Steele and Addison." P. 140.

[22] Compare the following famous paragraph in the Treatise:

> Most fortunately it happens that since reason is incapable of dispelling these clouds nature herself suffices to that purpose, and cures me of this philosophical melancholy and delirium, either by relaxing this bent of mind, or by some avocation, and lively impression of my senses which obliterate all these chimeras. I dine, I play a game of backgammon, I converse, and am merry with my friends; and when after three or four hours' amusement, I would return to these speculations, they appear so cold and strained, and ridiculous, that

I cannot find in my heart to enter into them any farther. (P. 269)

[23] Kemp Smith, op. cit., Chapters Two and Three.

[24] Ibid., p. 56.

[25] Rosalie Colie, "The Essayist in his Essay," in John Yolton, editor, John Locke: Problems and Perspectives (Cambridge: Cambridge University Press, 1969), pp. 234-261.

[26] Even in an essay with such an objective-sounding title as "That Politics May be Reduced to a Science," Shirley Letwin has shown how one of Hume's primary intentions was to moderate the partisan zeal of his day. See Letwin, op. cit., pp. 88-90.

[27] Enquiries, pp. 109-131.

[28] "Of Suicide," op. cit.

[29] Locke's Essay, II, XXIII, Par. 12.

[30] Medieval thought is philosophical in the sense that for medieval men all of man's activities had their appropriate niche in a hierarchy of being that both reflected and connected with a celestial hierarchy of being. See A.O. Lovejoy's classic work, The Great Chain of Being: A Study of the History of an Idea, Harper Torchbooks (New York: Harper and Row, 1960), Chapter Three. On the philosophical character of Renaissance thought, see Ernst Cassirer, The Individual and the Cosmos in Renaissance Philosophy, Harper Torchbooks (New York: Harper and Row, 1963).

[31] Treatise, p. 273. Compare Halevy: "In fact, though he is more of a dialectician and

analyst and less of a man of learning, Hume is in many respects the English Montaigne. To him associationism is a philosophy against the philosophers, a series of reasonings turned against reasoning itself, in a word, an irrationalism." Elie Halevy, <u>The Growth of Philosophic Radicalism</u>, Beacon Paperbacks (Boston: The Beacon Press, 1966), p. 10.

ABOUT THE AUTHOR

Aryeh Botwinick was educated at Yeshiva University, the London School of Economics and Princeton. He has taught at Swarthmore College, and is currently serving as an Assistant Professor of Political Science -- specializing in political philosophy -- at Temple University. Dr. Botwinick's major scholarly interests are the political philosophy of liberalism, methodological issues in the social sciences and the political economy of a society of scarcity. His articles have appeared in Auslegung, the Journal of Social Philosophy, the Journal of the History of Philosophy, Judaism and the Philosophy Forum. He is currently engaged in research for a projected two-volume work on Man and Society in an Age of Scarcity.